Thomas Schirrmacher

**Culture of Shame / Culture of Guilt**

# World of Theology Series

## Published by the Theological Commission of the World Evangelical Alliance

### Volume 6

Vol 1   Thomas K. Johnson: The First Step in Missions Training: How our Neighbors are Wrestling with God's General Revelation
Vol 2   Thomas K. Johnson: Christian Ethics in Secular Cultures
Vol 3   David Parker: Discerning the Obedience of Faith: A Short History of the World Evangelical Alliance Theological Commission (in preparation)
Vol 4   Thomas Schirrmacher (Ed.): William Carey: Theologian – Linguist – Social Reformer
Vol 5   Thomas Schirrmacher: Advocate of Love – Martin Bucer as Theologian and Pastor
Vol 6   Thomas Schirrmacher: Culture of Shame / Culture of Guilt – Applying the Word of God in Different Situations
Vol 7   Thomas Schirrmacher: The Koran and the Bible
Vol 8   Thomas Schirrmacher (Ed.): The Humanisation of Slavery in the Old Testament
Vol 9   Jim Harries: New Foundations for Appreciating Africa: Beyond Religious and Secular Deceptions
Vol 10  Thomas Schirrmacher: Missio Dei – God's Missional Nature
Vol 11  Thomas Schirrmacher: Biblical Foundations for 21st Century World Mission

Thomas Schirrmacher

# Culture of Shame / Culture of Guilt
## Applying the Word of God in Different Situations

Translator: Richard McClary
Editor: Thomas K. Johnson
Editorial Assistant: Ruth Baldwin

WIPF & STOCK · Eugene, Oregon

Wipf and Stock Publishers
199 W 8th Ave, Suite 3
Eugene, OR 97401

Culture of Shame, Culture of Guilt
Applying the Word of God in Different Situations
By Schirrmacher, Thomas
Copyright©2013 Verlag für Kultur und Wissenschaft
ISBN 13: 978-1-5326-5575-3
Publication date 4/17/2018
Previously published by Verlag für Kultur und Wissenschaft, 2013

# Contents

Foreword ............................................................................................. 7

1. **Preliminary Remarks** ................................................................. 9
2. **Classical Positions in Cultural Anthropology** .......................... 11
   Christine Schirrmacher: from the Viewpoint of Islamic Studies ....... 11
   Lothar Käser from the Ethnological Point of View ......................... 13
   Helm Stierlin from a Psychoanalytic Point of View ........................ 17
3. **On the history of Differentiating between Shame and Guilt Orientations** ............................................................................. 19
   Cultural Anthropology ..................................................................... 19
   Psychoanalysis and Psychology ....................................................... 24
   Cognitive Psychology ...................................................................... 27
   Sociology .......................................................................................... 27
   Missiology ........................................................................................ 28
   Theology and Ethics ......................................................................... 29
4. **Is the biblical message shame-oriented or guilt-oriented?** ........... 33
   Is western Christian theology a misguided development? ................ 33
   One must distinguish how one addresses the guilt-oriented or shame-oriented conscience from whether the biblical message is itself guilt-oriented or shame-oriented. .................................. 36
   One must distinguish between what was reported Old Testament Israel and in the New Testament church from what was and is the message and will of God. ......................................................... 37
   Biblical concepts may not simply be equated with modern concepts. ..................................................................................... 38
5. **Theses regarding the complementarity between shame and guilt orientations in the holy scriptures** ........................................... 41
   Guilt and feelings of guilt have to be distinguished, as do shame and feelings of shame. ................................................................. 41
   Sin leads to guilt – sin leads to shame ............................................. 42
   Guilt and shame have to orient themselves towards what God's Word considers to be sin, righteousness, and peace. .................. 44
   The primacy of God's glory makes it impossible to factor out aspects of honor and dishonor from Christian dogmatics and ethics! ........................................................................................ 44

No self-salvation means righteousness and honor/glory cannot be produced by men themselves.................................................. 46
The Mediator is the Judge. .............................................................. 47
Community Orientation = Shame Orientation = Covenant Orientation?................................................................................ 48
Community orientation does not automatically equate to a shame orientation............................................................................. 51
Individualism and collectivism ......................................................... 53
Respecters of the person and human rights...................................... 59
Against assimilation......................................................................... 61

6. **The Conscience Must orient itself towards God's Standard.** ........ 63

7. **Concluding Appeal** ............................................................................. 77

8. **Bibliography** ......................................................................................... 79

About the Author................................................................................... 87

# Foreword

Theology, as Thomas Schirrmacher has correctly realized, has until now hardly given adequate attention to the topic of the differences between those cultures which are primarily shame-oriented and those cultures which are primarily guilt-oriented. If nothing else, in newer Protestant theology and ethics this is bound up with an orientation towards the philosopher Immanuel Kant. In his ethics, which are oriented towards reason and moral standards recognized by reason, *feelings* have no place. Only the phenomenologically oriented philosophers such as Max Scheler and Paul Ricoeur have dealt with shame more closely. Surely theology's concentration on the topic of guilt has to do with the one-sided emphasis on guilt in theology that is western, or occidental, and above all medieval.

In developmental psychology, the meaning of shame in childhood development as well as in the life of adults has especially been seen and highlighted since Sigmund Freud. Partially due to this psychological viewpoint, cultural anthropologists have emphasized the differences between cultures and religions which are primarily shame-oriented and those which are primarily guilt-oriented. Since the prevailing number of cultures in Asia, Africa, and Latin America are shame-oriented, Christian missionaries have also encountered this complex of issues. In particular, those missionaries shaped by an occidental tradition of evangelically oriented missionary societies had to ask themselves how they could convey a primarily guilt-oriented Christian message in primarily shame-oriented cultures. This also led to the question of whether the biblical message is actually as guilt oriented as it had appeared within the western tradition. Some are now of the opinion that in the Bible the orientation towards shame is even stronger than the orientation towards guilt.

It is to Thomas Schirrmacher's credit that the work before you is not only intended for missiology and missionary activity, but also for religious education, ethics, and counseling from a cultural anthropological and theological point of view. It demonstrates that an opposition between shame and guilt, however, neither corresponds to the biblical message, nor does it correspond to western tradition and to churches with reformed backgrounds. It demonstrates rather, that aspects of shame are considered and integrated in both of these environments. The work at hand is a particular challenge to more closely clarify the indisputable differences between primarily shame-oriented and primarily guilt-oriented cultures in their importance for the Christian teachings of sin and reconciliation with God through Christ. There are contexts where one does not see the core of the biblical view of sin in particular acts of misconduct over against a moral norm, that is to say, in sinful acts. Rather, it is seen in a lack of faith, that is to say, in a wrong basic life orientation and in the corresponding breach of God's design for human life, which is to trust Him, to give him glory and honor, and to love Him and one's neighbor as oneself. Especially in such environments, shame reveals itself to be a significant dimension of sin and of recognizing sin, and embarrassment reveals itself to be an important aspect of becoming honest before God and with that, divine judgment.


Bonn, May 26, 2005
Prof. Dr. Ulrich Eibach
Professor for Systematic Theology, Bonn

# I. Preliminary Remarks

In recent times there have been two comprehensive investigations on the topic of shame and guilt orientation in culture and conscience penned by Evangelical, missiological authors. The first is a master's thesis by Martin Lomen in the German language.[1] The second is a dissertation by Hannes Wiher in the English language,[2] which we have published. Both of these works address the question of how the Christian gospel can be conveyed in shame-oriented societies. Wiher's dissertation received the George-W.-Peters Prize in 2005, which is an indication of the growing interest in this topic.

Lomen and Wiher come to the conclusion that in the Bible, guilt orientation and shame orientation balance each other out (in particular *Lohen*, pp. 157-160; and *Wiher, Shame*, pp. 280, 342, 215). Both hold that the predominant guilt orientation in western Christianity is an undesirable development. This point of view is not being advocated for the first time.[3] Yet it is found to be well summarized here. In Wiher it is addressed in academic breadth, while in Lomen it is treated with ethno-hermeneutic depth, both respectively in manners heretofore not conducted.

This topic has occupied me for several years. Here three fields of study in which I have completed doctoral work intersect. As a missiologist, the question of how the gospel can be communicated in cultures with completely different senses of justice is of central importance. As a cultural anthropologist, the differentiation between shame and guilt orientation is something with which I am theoretically and practically familiar. The question arises as to which concrete consequences this has for society and theology. And finally, as a systematic theologian, the question that arises is the ex-

---

[1] Martin Lomen. *Sünde und Scham im biblischen und islamischen Kontext: Ein ethno-hermeneutischer Beitrag zum christlich-islamischen Dialog.* Edition afem – mission scripts 21. Nürnberg: VTR, 2003 – hereafter referred to as *Lomen*.

[2] Hannes Wiher. *Shame and Guilt: A Key to Cross-Cultural Ministry.* Edition iwg – mission academics 10. Bonn: Verlag für Kultur und Wissenschaft, 2003 – hereafter referred to as *Wiher, Shame* in order to distinguish from an earlier investigation Hannes Wiher. *Missionsdienst in Guinea: Das Evangelium für eine schamorientierte, von Animismus und Volksislam geprägten Gesellschaft.* Edition afem, mission scripts 14. Bonn: Verlag für Kultur und Wissenschaft, 1998; French edition: Hannes Wiher. *L'Évangile et la Culture de Honte en Afrique Occidentale.* Edition iwg, mission scripts 21. Bonn: Verlag für Kultur und Wissenschaft, 2003.

[3] See the representatives referred to further below.

tent to which the biblical message and teaching tends more in one direction or the other. That is an important question that has to be clarified so that we do not confuse our dogmatic positions with the biblical message and fall into the danger of making our cultural orientation the norm for Christians in other cultures.

# 2. Classical Positions in Cultural Anthropology

I would like to begin by differentiating between shame orientation and guilt orientation. I will do this by referring to statements by classical representatives from the fields of Islamic studies, cultural anthropology, and psychology (psychoanalysis). This is deliberately done through the use of several longer quotations which speak for themselves.

## Christine Schirrmacher: from the Viewpoint of Islamic Studies

Christine Schirrmacher has done a good job commenting on the differences between shame and guilt orientations by using practical examples. She gives particular consideration to Islamic folk culture:

"Whoever wants to understand the unwritten societal rules of the Islamic world and in particular how the genders behave towards each other, their boundaries and room for maneuver, the reactions from the environment, and the laws that enable life together, has to become familiar with several basic principles of shame-oriented and guilt-oriented cultures as well as with understandings of 'honor and disgrace' in the context of the Near East.

If an individual – generalizing somewhat – assumes that in the western world there is a predominating guilt orientation, what is understood with this term is that guilt is sensed in an incident the moment it occurs. Cleansing from guilt occurs through an admission of guilt and, if possible, restitution. A direct confrontation between offender and victim is possible, and it is even desirable in the case of conflict. It brings about a discharging of, as well as, an end of the conflict: Whoever slams his car into his neighbor's car feels guilty at the moment the event occurs (even if it turns out that he flees the scene of the accident). The incident in itself causes guilt feelings, independent of the relationship with the neighbor, independent of whether the car is old or new, and independent of whether the neighbor was a witness to the accident or not. Settling the affair occurs when admission is made by the individual who caused the accident, and it might possibly contain an apology and restitution (coming up with funds to pay for the damages).

In a shame-oriented culture it is less the event itself that plays a role but rather the question of what relationship exists between the offender and the victim, and of how face can be saved in the presence of the other individual. If a command is violated that negatively affects a relationship between people, then reconciliation is what stands in the center and not the offense itself. How the accident is discussed and dealt with is dependent on the quality of the mutual relationship. If the neighbor is in debt to the individual who caused the accident, then the event will be played down. It might possibly be played down by making reference to the fact that the vehicle was worthless and that there is poor visibility in the street. Under certain circumstances the individual who caused the accident might not even be allowed to pay damages. If such action is taken, the 'give and take' between neighbors is balanced out. The victim might even be glad that an opportunity has thereby been offered to remove the debt owed to the neighbor. Cleansing guilt or offsetting a debt that comes with neglecting an incident can occur by a good deed from the other party, possibly one already conducted in advance.

If the individual who caused the accident was already indebted, then the victim can treat the accident as a personal attack, demand excessive compensation for damages, and under certain circumstances 'put the relationship on ice' for a longer period of time until an opportunity for reconciliation arises. When it comes time for a religious celebration, such as a celebration that occurs when a fast is broken, there might be, for instance, a renewed opportunity for reconciliation for the individual who caused the accident, such that a give and take offset can be achieved.

In a shame oriented culture, the 'give and take' between relatives and friends, indeed between everyone who finds himself in a relationship (including an official with a governmental authority who has been asked to conduct an official act) has to always remain in an approximate state of balance. If, for example, a petitioner does not have a relationship with an official and is unable to build a relationship via a third party, that individual often has only little hope for help and fulfillment of his request.

Whoever has done a very large favor for a friend, or even a number of favors, has to a certain extent made a 'deposit' into an account with the friend. If the individual falls into trouble, he can rest assured that he will receive help from his friend. Indeed it is practically his moral right. This friend is so deeply obligated to the person making the request that to reject a plea is as good as impossible and would be strongly disapproved of. He has to do everything within his power to provide the assistance.

If the individual does not, however, wish to provide the assistance, for reasons which possibly are in turn due to obligations towards other people that weigh more heavily – that is to say, there is a conflict of loyalties – the indebted individual will conduct an evasion maneuver. However, he will in

## 2. Classical Positions in Cultural Anthropology

no way confront the petitioner with a flat 'no.' A request, according to a rule of societal life in a shame-oriented culture, be it justified or unjustified, should never be refused directly.

The individual may withdraw from the petitioner, in that for a while he is not to be found or produces excuses and reasons why at the moment he is prevented by numerous difficulties, or why the fulfillment of the request has to be postponed. Often both parties know that this is a refusal, which, however, is not openly made a topic of discussion as such. In this manner neither the petitioner nor the individual who rejects the plea loses face. Indeed, the request can be fulfilled at a later time – when the preconditions for the possibility of fulfillment present themselves – since an official 'no' was never given.

If dishonor is brought to a blameless person, the individual can demand reconciliation. This should, however, always be sought within a framework that allows the other party to save face. Such a situation occurs often, for example, when a victim of a theft does not turn directly on the thief but to his relatives. What can take place is that the point of contention does not even arise in a discussion, and the perpetrators are not the target of embarrassment. Rather, a circuitous indication is given about what happened. This is how reconciliation occurs without naming the incident clearly and shaming the person who is the cause. As a general rule, to put the other person in a bad light is viewed to be worse than the offense itself.

In a shame-oriented culture, what is considered to be appropriate behavior is not decided by an individual but rather by the society as a whole. It is a collective matter. For that reason each individual acts with regard to what consequences there are for the group, the family, and the society.

In a guilt-oriented culture, individual behavior that varies from case to case can be tolerated. For the most part, decisions have meaning for the individual and are not blamed on a group, the family, and society."[4]

### Lothar Käser from the Ethnological Point of View

The Christian-oriented ethnologist, Lothar Käser, who is based in Freibourg, has given classic definitions of guilt orientation and shame orientation in his textbook.[5] Basically, he proceeds on the assumption of distinct feelings of guilt and shame:

---

[4] Christine Schirrmacher. *Kleines Lexikon der islamischen Familie*. Holzgerlingen: Hänssler, 2002. pp. 58-66 (Quote revised by the author).

[5] Lothar Käser. *Fremde Kulturen: Eine Einführung in die Ethnologie*. VLM: Lahr & Verlag der Evang.-Luth. Mission: Erlangen, 1998². Chapter 10. "Kultur und Über-Ich (Gewissen)", pp. 129-167, in part. 166; comp. on this Wiher, Shame 112-116.

> "Guilt feelings are, as a general rule, reactions of the conscience, with which the individual reacts to infractions of norms that have been expressly formulated in his culture, society, or group as *justice* and *laws*. This can take the form of ordinances in written form (a civil code, a set of traffic regulations), but also simply a verbal agreement (a promise to hold a lecture that then has to be kept). Guilt feelings are also reactions of conscience with which an individual reacts to infractions of norms about which he knows that they have been put in place by an extra-human authority, a divinity, for instance. Such infringements are called *sin*, a term, by the way, that is not only found in Christian culture.
>
> In contrast, while feelings of shame are, as a general rule, reactions of conscience with which an individual reacts to infractions of norms, these norms are generally viewed as accepted rules of *decency, civilized behavior,* or *good conduct*. Furthermore, they are seen as things that are simply to be done and what 'one' should strive for. This might include table manners, codes of dress, a certain body weight that should not be exceeded, or the ability to reach a certain level of athletic achievement which is similarly achieved by other members of the group."[6]

This differentiation does not only shape the individual, but rather entire cultures:

> "If a person investigates different cultures, societies, and groups on the basis of what they have in common and where they differ, there are *two basic forms* that the orientation of human conscience can take. There are cultures, societies, and groups whose individuals predominantly are *guilt-oriented*, and there are cultures, societies, and groups whose individuals predominantly react in a *shame-oriented* manner. (One should note that the emphasis is on "predominantly"!) Put bluntly: there are cultures, societies, and groups with individuals whose consciences are predominantly punished by guilt feelings when they infringe upon norms, and there are such where individuals' consciences are predominantly punished by feelings of shame. From both of these criteria, there arise profound differences in behavior among people and, naturally, for the whole culture as well."[7]

These different alignments lead to diverse structures in society.

> "Societies with individuals who tend to be more guilt-oriented are generally narrowly structured and normalized. They allow a pluralism of opinions and tend to a diversity of values and behavioral patterns. Because the *freedom of the individual* receives a higher value, they tend to be threatened with disin-

---

[6] Lothar Käser. *Fremde Kulturen. op. cit.*, p. 138.
[7] Käser, p. 139.

## 2. Classical Positions in Cultural Anthropology 15

tegration. This is due to the fact that what is granted to the individual is the right to hold their own opinions and needs to be more important than those of 'others.' When it comes to decisions that necessitate a common belief, a discussion is normally conducted only for as long as it takes to reach a recognizable majority.

Societies with individuals who tend to be more shame-oriented are more narrowly structured and often are strictly hierarchical. They tend towards a harmony of opinions, values, and behavioral patterns. Their members view themselves as more forced to subordinate their individual freedom, their opinions, and their needs to the interests of the group. They are less important than 'the others.' When it comes to decisions that require mutual agreement, a discussion usually lasts as long as it takes for all the participants to come on board with the solution that is found. (Europeans have invented the label *palaver* for this occasionally rather tedious process.)[8]

On the basis of these structural differences, the dissemination of guilt orientation and shame orientation also can be culturally historically affixed, even if Käser, when he goes into detail, refers to the necessity of allowing for a broad differentiation.

"The type of culture with a predominant guilt orientation is primarily found in complex, industrially shaped European western societies. It is, however, to be observed that this applies in particular to society's upper classes and to the urban milieu. In their lower classes and in the rural setting, shame orientation is comparatively more clearly pronounced. The spread of the principle of guilt orientation appears to overlap with those areas in which Christianity took the shape of the leading religious form, or where at least the basic societal forms were defined by it (the 'Christian west'). The relationships were, however, not quite so simple. One needs to guard against generalizations of this type.

The type of culture that predominantly has a shame orientation, on the other hand, is found in less complex societies, ones that have less written and more oral tradition in the foundations of their ethnic groupings. These include hunter-gatherers, planters, farmers, and cattle breeders, but possibly also such complex modern industrial societies as those of the Japanese or Chinese."[9]

Käser's former colleague on the Truk Islands, the missiologist Klaus W. Müller, has produced a good comparison:

---

[8] Käser, p. 140.
[9] Käser, p. 140.

| Guilt and Shame Orientation | |
|---|---|
| based on Klaus W. Müller's work[10] | |
| *Guilt-oriented* | *Shame-oriented* |
| **Starting Point for the Shaping of Orientation** | |
| A small number of individuals who are formative influences, defined precisely: parents (nuclear family) | A large number of individuals who are formative influences, imprecisely defined: parents and relatives, strangers, spirits |
| **Structure** | |
| Behavioral standards are acquired from people who are formative influences and the conscience is trained. | Behavioral standards are acquired from people who are formative influences and the conscience is trained. |
| **Manifestation of Orientation** | |
| Within the individual, as one's own conscience performs the monitoring of norms. | Other individuals or spirits are the authorities which perform the monitoring of norms. |
| **Reaction to a planned Norm Infraction** | |
| The conscience signals that the imagined act is wrong. Defense mechanism is activated. | The conscience signals that the imagined act is wrong. Defense mechanism is activated. |
| **Reaction to an actual Norm Infraction** | |
| A disturbance of balance caused within. An immediate guilt feeling is experienced that is sensed to be punishment. Relief mechanism is activated. | A disturbance of balance from without, but only if the act is known to others. An immediate feeling that is always one of shame and is sensed to be punishment. Defense mechanism is activated Relief mechanism is activated. |
| **Results** | |
| An operational conscience (superego) leads to peace. | An operational conscience (superego) leads to peace. |

---

[10] Presented in a slightly different graphical form and quoted from Klaus W. Müller. "Elenktik: Gewissen im Kontext." pp. 416-451 in: Hans Kasdorf, Klaus W. Müller (eds.). *Bilanz und Plan: Mission an der Schwelle zum Dritten Jahrtausend. Festschrift für George W. Peters zu seinem achtzigsten Geburtstag.* Bad Liebenzell: Verlag der Liebenzeller Mission, 1988, p. 439.

## 2. Classical Positions in Cultural Anthropology

## Helm Stierlin from a Psychoanalytic Point of View

The Heidelberg psychoanalyst and family therapist Helm Stierlin has summarized the state of psychological research as follows:

> "Shame and guilt are essential elements of human experience and therefore also essential to psychiatric theory and practice. They occupy philosophers such as Kierkegaard, Nietzsche, Sartre, Heidegger, and Jaspers, and psychoanalysts such as Freud and Erikson. In both cases one is dealing with painful and complex emotions. They interlock but are different according to their phenomenology and dynamics.... Several psychoanalytic authors have described differences and similarities relating to both phenomena. By virtue of this, shame and guilt differ in spite of their similarities with respect to linguistic usage and linguistic origin. Shame implies painful embarrassment and a very deep feeling of anxiety and humiliation such that one would like to 'sink into the ground.' This feeling of becoming small is contrasted with uplifting feelings, such as those of pride and triumph, which convey the antitheses of shame."[11]

How do shame and guilt differ from each other?

> "Shame grows primarily out of defeat in competition, from rejection and the feeling of having lost self-control and of an accompanying sense of having lost one's self esteem. Shame often accompanies the feeling of having a bodily or sexual deficiency. A girl, for example, is ashamed of having small breasts, of being sexually frigid (either apparently or actually), or of having an all too strong readiness for becoming aroused (in her eyes a weakness). A boy is ashamed of his impotence, of his (in his eyes) small penis or of his lack of sexual experience. In German the word *Schamteile* (translator's addition: German for genitals and consisting of the words for shame – *Scham* – and parts – *Teile*), reflects the close affinity between sexual function, anatomy, and shame. With guilt, in contrast, we suffer pain because we have inflicted damage upon other people or sacrosanct institutions such as family, church, or our homeland (allegedly or actually). Specifically, guilt arises in situations in which we (in fact or as a figment of our imagination) attack, deceive, manipulate, humiliate, or begrudge those we appear to love or desire to love. In summary we can use a phrase from Piers and Singer and say: 'Guilt-fear emerges as a result of a violation, while shame arises out of failure.'"[12]

---

[11] Helm Stierlin. *Adolf Hitler: Familienperspektiven*. Suhrkamp taschenbuch 2361. Frankfurt: Suhrkamp, new edition 1995 (1975). p. 109.
[12] *Stierlin*, pp. 109-110.

Stierlin next joins shame and guilt with Freud's teaching:

> "Freud's concepts of the ego-ideal and the superego throw light upon the dynamic processes at hand. According to Freud, the tension between the ego and the ego-ideal (or the superego) is reflected in guilt and shame. The essence of these tensions resolved themselves for Freud when in 1933 he differentiated between the three superego functions of the ego-ideal, the conscience, and self-observation. In the process, above all the ego-ideal played a role in shame, the conscience a role in guilt, while self-observation was employed in shame and guilt, albeit in different ways.
>
> Pursuant to this concept of the superego, shame emerges if we do not satisfy the demands of the ego-ideal. This is to say, if we are not as strong, beautiful, confident, competent, or sexually potent as the ego-ideal demands. Guilt is generated when we act counter to a conscience that forbids injuring, deceiving, humiliating, or disappointing those whom we owe love and respect. (thus the graphic German term *Gewissensbiss* – literally, a bite in the conscience).
>
> Self-observation as a third superego function is tied to shame and guilt as well. In the meaning intended here, it includes the estimation and judgment, respectively, of our self as well as the selves of others and the entire situation. Understood thusly, self-observation decides the degree to which we deviate from the ego-ideal or conscience in our actions and desires. Such self-observation varies, where strictness and astuteness are concerned, from individual to individual. With one individual it appears strong, extraordinarily concentrated, and relentless and with others, in contrast, it is weak, diffused, and compliant. Furthermore – and this is important here – it can be suspended, perverted, or circumvented, which thereby enables the individual to more or less evade the pain of shame or guilt. This defensive use (or non-use) of self-observation then affects the dynamic processes which typically come into operation with shame and guilt in order to mitigate pain.
>
> In the case of (actual or potential) shame, the individual attempts to massively block self-observation: the person closes his eyes to the action performed, hides, or wants what has happened to be undone by living in denial of it. In the case of (actual or potential) guilt, the individual attempts to hush the voice of conscience by distorting perception and twisting responsibility, above all with the aid of projection. As a result, the individual at least temporarily attempts to cast off guilt by accusing or punishing others as is described in the psychoanalytic literature of Freud (1926), Fenichel (1945, 1954) et al. At the same time, it often unknowingly leads to a situation in which the individual accuses or punishes himself."[13]

---

[13] *Stierlin*, pp. 110-111.

## 3. On the history of Differentiating between Shame and Guilt Orientations

### Cultural Anthropology

It is good to follow the history of research with respect to differentiating between orientations towards shame and guilt in psychology and cultural anthropology. This has been traced out in the new investigations conducted by Martin Lomen and Hannes Wiher,[14] even if there are numerous details to add and even if one finds that other fields of specialization, such as sociology, are in large part missing. We want to briefly trace this history of research and in the process add a number of supplements to Lomen and Wiher, all before we bring this home with two classic presentations.

No doubt in part inspired by investigations having to do with the importance of shame in psychology and psychoanalysis, the difference between orientations toward shame and guilt[15] became a topic in cultural anthropology.[16] Margaret Mead, who studied psychology and cultural anthropology, made a beginning with her description of Indian peoples in 1937.[17] Better known was Ruth Benedict, who in 1946 described in detail how the Japanese culture is a shame culture in which the guilt question

---

[14] Wiher 60-160 and often; briefly in Lomen 18-22; comp. 38-74.
[15] Up into the 50s one generally spoke rather absolutely of a 'shame culture' or a 'guilt culture.' Since that time increasingly strong formulations are used that make it clear that shame and guilt feelings are found everywhere, and that what is more at issue is the question of what prevails.
[16] Comp the overview on the research history in *Wiher, Shame* 103-132, above all regarding the first representatives 103-105.
[17] Margret Mead (ed.). *Cooperation and Competition Among Primitive Peoples*, New York: McGraw-Hill Book Company, 1937; revised edition. Boston: Beacon Press, 1961. Reference to Mead is missing in *Lomen* 18, who first addresses Ruth Benedict 1946; comp., however, *Wiher, Shame* 103-105. In her autobiography Margaret Mead. *Brombeerblüten im Winter: Ein befreites Leben*. rororo 4226. Reinbek: Rowohlt, 1989 (1978 reprint) (English 1972) Mead unfortunately does not go into how she acquired her view. On Mead's research in general comp. Noa Vera Zanolli. "Margaret Mead (1901-1978)." pp. 295-314 in: Wolfgang Marschall (ed.). *Klassiker der Kulturanthropologie: Von Montaigne bis Margaret Mead*. München: C. H. Beck, 1990, as well as pp. 361-364 by her and about her and pp. 299-300 on the relationship to Benedict and Boas. Mead has been intensely criticized by Derek Freeman. *Liebe ohne Aggression: Margaret Meads Legende von der Friedfertigkeit der Naturvölker*. Kindler: München, 1983.

does not play a role.[18] Both were students[19] of the distinguished ethnologist Franz Boas,[20] who viewed culture as a functional whole. He put an end to cultural evolutionism, and in the USA he established the integrated science of cultural anthropology as a synopsis of all areas of a society.[21]

---

[18] Ruth Benedict. *The Chrysanthenum and the Sword: Patterns of Japanese Culture.* Boston: Houghton and Mifflin, 1946. Comp. on Japanese shame-oriented culture from a later time Shinobu S. Kitayama (ed.). *Emotion and Culture: Empirical Studies of Mutual Influence.* Washington, DC: American Psychological Association Press, 1994; C. Norman Kraus. "The Cross of Christ – Dealing with Shame and Guilt". *Japan Christian Quarterly* 53 (1987): 221-227; Takie Sugiyama Lebra. "On social mechanisms of guilt and shame": The Japanese Case." *Antropolocial Quarterly* 44 (1971): 241-245; (later, however, more critical:) Takie Sugiyama Lebra. "Shame and Guilt: A Psychocultural View of the Japanese Self." *Ethos: Journal of the Society for Psychological Anthropology* 2 (1983) 3: 192-209; additional literature on Japan in: Wolfgang Blankenburg. "Zur Differenzierung von Scham und Schuld". pp. 45-56 in: Rolf Kühn, Michael Raub. Michael Titze (eds.). *Scham – ein menschliches Gefühl: Kulturelle, psychologische und philosophische Perspektiven.* Köln: Westdeutscher Verlag, 1997. p. 46 and p. 46, Note 6.

[19] On Benedict as Boas' student comp. Ruth Benedict. "Religion". pp. 627-665 in: Franz Boas (ed.). *General Anthropology. War Department Educational Manual 226.* Boston (USA): Heath / Madison (WI): US Armed Forces Inst., 1938; 1944; reprint: New York: Johnson, 1965. critical statements on Benedict's research: Ronald C. Johnson et al., "Guilt, Shame and adjustment in three cultures." *Personality and Individual Differences 8* (1987) 3: 357-364. On Mead as Boas' student comp. Margaret Mead. "Apprenticeship Under Boas." pp. 29-45 in: Walter Goldschmidt (ed.). *The Anthropology of Franz Boas: Essays on the Centennial of His Birth.* Washington, D.C., The American Anthropological Association, 1959 comp. from a later time against Mead's research Derek Freeman. *Liebe ohne Aggression: Margaret Meads Legende von der Friedfertigkeit der Naturvölker.* Kindler: München, 1983 and Walter Krämer et al. *Das neue Lexikon der populären Irrtümer.* Eichborn: Frankfurt, 1998. pp. 290-291. Comp. also more generally against Mead's view that 'primitive' peoples ´were harmonious: Robert B. Edgerton. *Sick Societies: Challenging the Myth of Primitive Harmony.* The Free Press: New York, 1992 und Colin M. Turnbull. *Das Volk ohne Liebe: Der soziale Untergang der Ik.* Rowohlt: Reinbek, 1973.

[20] Comp. from Boas above all. Franz Boas. *Race, Language and Culture.* New York: The Macmillan Comp., 1948 (collected essays); Franz Boas (ed.). *General Anthropology. War Department Educational Manual 226.* Boston (USA): Heath / Madison (WI): US Armed Forces Inst., 1938; 1944; reprint: New York: Johnson, 1965. Comp. on Boas the essays in Walter Goldschmidt (ed.). *The Anthropology of Franz Boas: Essays on the Centennial of His Birth.* Washington, D.C., The American Anthropological Association, 1959.

[21] For instance Roland Girtler. *Kulturanthropologie.* dtv wissenschaft. dtv: München, 1979. pp. 34-37.

## 3. On the history of Differentiating between Shame and Guilt Orientations

Similar observations and classifications were perceived by cultural anthropologists or missionaries who were laboring cultural-anthropologically with the Chinese,[22] the Indian[23], the Korean[24], the Javan[25], the Kurdish[26], the Arab-Near Eastern[27] and Islamic[28], the Mexican-Indian[29] and the Medi-

---

[22] Wolfram Eberhard. *Guilt and Sin in Traditional China.* Berkeley (USA): University of California Press, 1967; Deborah Stipek. "Differences between Americans and Chinese in the circumstances evoking pride, shame, and guilt". *Journal of Cross-cultural Psychology 29* (1998) 5: 616-629.

[23] See the essays in Shinobu S. Kitayama (ed.). *Emotion and Culture: Empirical Studies of Mutual Influence.* Washington, DC: American Psychological Association Press, 1994.

[24] Zuk-Nae Lee. "Koreanische Kultur und Schamgefühl." pp. 75-86 in: Rolf Kühn, Michael Raub. Michael Titze (eds.). *Scham – ein menschliches Gefühl: Kulturelle, psychologische und philosophische Perspektiven.* Köln: Westdeutscher Verlag, 1997.

[25] Ward Keeler. "Shame and Stage Fright in Java". *Ethos: Journal of the Society for Psychological Anthropology 2* (1983) 3: 152-165 (however with strong reservations).

[26] Denise L. Sweetnam. *Kurdish Culture: A Cross-Cultural Guide. Untersuchungen zur kurdischen Sprache und Kultur 4.* Bonn: VKW, 2004². pp. 59-114.

[27] Richard Buda, Sayed M. Elsayed-Elkhouly. "Cultural Differences between Arabs and Americans: Individualism-Collectivism Revisited". *Journal of Cross-Cultural Psychology 29* (1998) 3: 487-492.

[28] Comp. Martin Lomen. *Sünde und Scham im biblischen und islamischen Kontext: Ein ethno-hermeneutischer Beitrag zum christlich-islamischen Dialog.* Edition afem – mission scripts 21. Nürnberg: VTR, 2003. pp. 86-105 and the referred to Literature pp. 86-87; in addition Christine Schirrmacher. *Kleines Lexikon der islamischen Familie.* Holzgerlingen: Hänssler, 2002. Eintrag "Ehre und Schande", pp. 58-67; from the same author. *Herausforderung Islam.* Holzgerlingen: Hänssler, 2002. Chapter entitles "Terroranschläge gegen den Ehrverlust", pp. 72-86; Ismael Abu-Saad. "Individualism and Islamic Work Beliefs". *Journal of Cross-Cultural Psychology 29* (1998) 2: 377-383; Richard Buda, Sayed M. Elsayed-Elkhouly. "Cultural Differences between Arabs and Americans: Individualism-Collectivism Revisited." *Journal of Cross-Cultural Psychology 29* (1998) 3: 487-492; Roland Muller. *Honor and Shame: Unlocking the Door.* Philadelphia (PA): Xlibris Publications, 2000. pp. 79-99.

[29] Hanna-Maria Schmalenbach. "Die Lüge als Überlebensstrategie in schamorientierten und furchtbestimmten Kulturen." Mexico Report June 2002: 17-23 as a summary by Hanna-Maria Schmalenbach. "Die Lüge als Überlebensstrategie: Gedanken und Erfahrungen aus einer Missionsarbeit in Mexico." Unpublished Unveröffentlichte term paper. Columbia International University German Campus, Korntal, 2001.

terranean[30] cultures, which were all perceived as shame-oriented – and practically always in contrast to the western world.

In particular it was the influential Oxford classical philologist Eric Robertson Dodds who introduced the differentiation between shame cultures and guilt cultures in 1951.[31] He did this by presenting the old Greek civilization as a shame culture contrasted with the (at his time) modern world.[32]

It was not by chance that in 1953 a psychoanalyst and a cultural anthropologist, Gerhart Piers and Milton B. Singer, joined forces to write the first cross-cultural standard work on the topic.[33] Measured against its later influence, the book is astoundingly short and in the end, with respect to the entire concept, even cautiously critical.

> "Gerhart Piers delivered the psychoanalytic model, which was then applied in the area of anthropology by Milton B. Singer. In the process, Piers differentiated between the *superego*, that produces guilt, and the *ego-ideal*, which produces shame. The *superego* orients itself towards a set of rules and upon an infraction of the rules punishes the ego with a feeling of guilt. The *ego-ideal*, on the contrary, orients itself toward an internalized ideal and punishes the ego with a feeling of shame when the ego does not achieve the ideal." (Lomen 18-19)

A highly interesting study on the topic of shame and guilt, from the vantage point of the crossroads of cultural anthropology and psychology / educational science, was authored by Melford Spiro in his 1958 study on rai-

---

[30] Comp. Jean G. Peristiany (ed.). *Honor and Shame: The Values of a Mediterranean Society*. London: Weidenfeld and Nicolson, 1965; Chicago: University of Chicago, 1966 (= 1970; 1974); David D. Gilmore (ed.). *Honour and Shame and the Unity of the Mediterranean*. AAA Special Publication 22. Washington: American Anthropological Association, 1987.

[31] Eric Robertson Dodds. *Die Griechen und das Irrationale*. Wissenschaftliche Buchgesellschaft: Darmstadt, 1970$^1$; 1976$^2$; reprint 1991 (original: *The Greeks and the Irrational*, Berkeley: Univ. of California Press, 1951; 15$^{th}$ printing 1984), therein parts. "Von der Schamkultur zur Schuldkultur". pp. 17-37. *Ibid.*, p. 175, Note 106 refers to Dodds on Ruth Benedict.

[32] Comp. Wiher, *Shame*, 38+303, there also successor Dodds in the judgement of antiquity; also later on it Philipp Steger. "Die Scham in der griechisch-römischen Antike." pp. 57-74 in: Rolf Kühn, Michael Raub. Michael Titze (eds.). *Scham – ein menschliches Gefühl: Kulturelle, psychologische und philosophische Perspektiven*. Köln: Westdeutscher Verlag, 1997.

[33] Gerhart Piers, Milton B. Singer. Shame and Guilt: *A Psychoanalytic and Cultural Study*. Springfield (IL): Charles C. Thomas, 1953; New York: Norton, 1971.

## 3. On the history of Differentiating between Shame and Guilt Orientations

sing children in a kibbutz in Israel.[34] In the study he comes to the conclusion that an orientation towards shame increases with the number of attachment figures an individual has.

A cultural anthropological anthology dating from 1965, which contained articles from a conference held in 1959, is what finally made the complex of problems surrounding shame and guilt a standard topic of ethnology.[35]

However, it should be noted that the differentiation between an orientations towards shame and an orientation towards guilt is everything but undisputed.[36]

---

[34] Melford E. Spiro. *The Children of the Kibbutz: A study in child training and personality.* Cambridge (MS): Harvard University Press, 1958; revised edition. 1975.

[35] Jean G. Peristiany (ed.). *Honor and Shame: The Values of a Mediterranean Society.* London: Weidenfeld and Nicolson, 1965; Chicago: University of Chicago, 1966 (= 1970; 1974); comp. later independent anthology John George Peristiany, Julian Pitt-Rivers (eds.). *Honour and Grace in Anthropology.* Cambridge: Cambridge University Press, 1992; Cambridge University Press – Digital Printing, 1999. Lomen and Wiher date this one year later in the in the American edition, yet the actual conference was published in London. One can name additionally as anthologies above all David D. Gilmore (ed.). *Honour and Shame and the Unity of the Mediterranean.* AAA Special Publication 22. Washington: American Anthropological Association, 1987.

[36] Among the most important critics there is: Ward Keeler. "Shame and Stage Fright in Java". *Ethos: Journal of the Society for Psychological Anthropology 2* (1983) 3: 152-165; Takie Sugiyama Lebra. "Shame and Guilt: A Psychocultural View of the Japanese Self." *Ethos: Journal of the Society for Psychological Anthropology 2* (1983) 3: 192-209; David P. Ausubel. *Theory and Problems of Child Development.* New York: Grune & Stratton, 1958$^1$; 1970$^2$; 1980$^3$; David P. Ausubel, Edmund V. Sullivan. *Das Kindesalter: Fakten, Probleme, Theorie.* München: Juventa Verlag, 1974 (part. p. 507); Douglas Graham. *Moral Learning and Development.* London: Batsdorf, 1972; Rolf Kühn, Michael Raub. Michael Titze (eds.). *Scham – ein menschliches Gefühl: Kulturelle, psychologische und philosophische Perspektiven.* Köln: Westdeutscher Verlag, 1997; Wolfgang Blankenburg. "Zur Differenzierung von Scham und Schuld". pp. 45-56 in: Rolf Kühn, Michael Raub. Michael Titze (eds.). *Scham – ein menschliches Gefühl: Kulturelle, psychologische und philosophische Perspektiven.* Köln: Westdeutscher Verlag, 1997; Ronald T. Potter-Efron. *Shame, Guilt and Alcoholism: Treatment Issues in Clinical Practice.* New York, London: Haworth Press, 1989; Patricia und Ronald Potter-Efron. *Schamgefühle verstehen und überwinden.* Heyne: München, 1992 (English edition. *Letting Go of Shame.* Minnesota (USA): Hazelden Foundation, 1989).

## Psychoanalysis and Psychology

Since Sigmund Freud[37] moved shame into the center of psychological interest as one of the basic human feelings[38] and differentiated it from feelings of guilt, there have been a number of scientific investigations on the topic of 'shame.'[39]

Sighard Neckel extended the antecedent history beyond Freud back to Darwin,[40] who viewed the sense of shame as something that appeared at the early stages of human development and that at a later time joined with feelings of guilt. According to Neckel, Freud took up this differentiation, which then in turn played a role with those cultural anthropologists who started with Freud as well as with all psychoanalysis. This was the case, in particular, with both of the so-called 'orthodox' members of the Freudian school who have been named, Mead and Benedict.[41] From there sociology,

---

[37] Till Bastian, Micha Hilgers. "Scham als Teil des Minderwertigkeitsgefühls – und die fehlende Theorie der Affekte." *Internationale Zeitschrift für Individualpsychologie 16* (1991): 102-110 criticize, however, that after 90 years of psychoanalysis "a theory of emotions" is still missing and join with Leon Wurmser. *Die Flucht vor dem Gewissen*. Heidelberg: Springer, 1987. S. 15, who wrote: "The emotions have to be given a special and independent role." Guilty for the treatment as unwanted stepchildren is Freud himself, who hardly addresses shame and where he does, only in a negative manner [Till Bastian, Micha Hilgers. "Kain – Die Trennung von Scham und Schuld am Beispiel der Genesis." *Psyche 44* (1990): 1100-1112, here p. 1106]. In order to avoid the charge of being unscientific, he apparently develops scientific models of the life of our drives but leaves leaves out difficult to understand feelings such as shame (Till Bastian, Micha Hilgers. "Scham als Teil des Minderwertigkeitsgefühls." pp. 102-103).

[38] Comp. with Freud as a starting point of the discussion on shame and guilt, e.g., Freud: "Die Bedeutung der Scham in der Seelsorge: Scham – die Nachseite der Liebe." Dissertation – Theologie: Bonn, 2002. pp. 50-51; Sighard Neckel. *Status und Scham: Zur symbolischen Reproduktion sozialer Ungleichheit. Theorie und Gesellschaft 21*. Frankfurt: Campus, 1991. pp. 46-49. Comp. basically to Freud's view of guilt feelings and feelings of shame Joseph Sandler. "Zum Begriff des Überichs." pp. 45-81 in: Karola Brede (ed.). *Das Überich und die Macht seiner Objekte: [50 Jahre Psyche]*. Stuttgart: Verlag Internationale Psychoanalyse, 1996; Melvin R. Lansky, Andrew P. Morrison. "The Legacy of Freud's Writings on Shame." pp. 3-40 in: Melvin R. Lansky, Andrew P. Morrison (eds.). *The Widening Scope of Shame*. Hillsdale (NJ): The Analytic Press, 1997.

[39] Comp. R. L. Timpe. "Shame." pp. 1074-1075 in: David G. Benner (ed.). *Baker's Encyclopedia of Psychology*. Grand Rapids (MI): Baker Books, 1985.

[40] Sighard Neckel. *Status und Scham*. pp. 42-44; comp. overall pp. 41-58.

[41] Comp. on the importance of Freud for cultural anthropology Mario Erdheim. "Sigmund Freud (1856-1939)." pp. 137-150 in: Wolfgang Marschall (ed.). *Klassi-*

psychology, and psychoanalysis assumed this differentiation.[42] For instance, in 1948 the psychoanalyst Franz Alexander taught that guilt was sensed on account of wrong action, while shame, on the other hand, was sensed on account of a feeling of inferiority.[43] In 1955 David P. Ausubel made the topic known in *Psychological Review*,[44] even though he later viewed the differentiation between shame and guilt very critically.[45] In 1953 there was a joint study by Gerhart Piers and Milton B. Singer,[46] which worked off the basis of Piers' psychoanalytic model. This study was mentioned earlier as having been done in connection with cultural anthropology. Helen Merell Lynds standard work on shame[47] was also influential, even if orientations toward shame and guilt only came up among other topics. In Helen B. Lewis' work from 1971 this was explicitly treated as a topic.[48] In the 1980s and above all in the 1990s a large number of comprehensive works on shame appeared, almost all of which also expressed a view on the complex of issues surrounding shame and guilt.[49] A good cross-section is offered by a 1995 anthology.[50]

---

  ker der Kulturanthropologie: Von Montaigne bis Margaret Mead. München: C. H. Beck, 1990.
[42] Comp. on the research history *Wiher, Shame* 60-102 and "Schuld/Schuldgefühle". pp. 242-247 in: *Lexikon der Bioethik*. 3 vols. vol. 3. Gütersloher Verlagshaus: Gütersloh, 1998. pp. 246-247.
[43] Franz Alexander. *Fundamentals of Psychoanalysis*. New York: Norton, 1948¹; 1963².
[44] David P. Ausubel. "Relationships between Shame and Guilt in the Socializing Process." *Psychological Review 62* (1955): 378-390.
[45] See David P. Ausubel. *Theory and Problems of Child Development*. New York: Grune & Stratton, 1958¹; 1970²; 1980³; David P. Ausubel, Edmund V. Sullivan. *Das Kindesalter: Fakten, Probleme, Theorie*. München: Juventa Verlag, 1974.
[46] Gerhart Piers, Milton B. Singer. *Shame and Guilt: A Psychoanalytic and Cultural Study*. Springfield (IL): Charles C. Thomas, 1953; New York: Norton, 1971.
[47] Helen Merell Lynd. *On Shame and the Search of Identity*. London: Routledge and Kegan Paul, 1958; New York: Science Editions, 1961.
[48] Helen B. Lewis. *Shame and Guilt in Neurosis*. New York: International Universities Press, 1971.
[49] Gershen Kaufman. *The Psychology of Shame: Theory and Treatment of Shame-Based Syndromes*. New York: Springer, 1989: comp. Gershen Kaufman. *Shame: The Power of Caring*. Cambridge, MA: Schenckman. 1980¹; 1992²; Gershen Kaufman, L. Rapahel. "Shame: A Perspective on Jewish Identity." *Journal of Psychology and Judaism 11* (1987): 30-40 and about Kaufman *Wiher, Shame* 73-75; Micha Hilgers. *Scham: Geschichte eines Affekts*. Göttingen: Vandenhoeck & Ruprecht, 1996¹; 1997²; Mario Jacoby. *Scham–Angst und Selbstwertgefühl: Ihre Bedeutung in der Psychotherapie*. Walter-Verlag: Olten (CH)/Freiburg, 1991; Francis J. Broucek. *Shame and the Self*. New York: The Guilford Press, 1991; Donald L. Nathanson (ed.). *The Many Faces of Shame*. New York: Guilford Press, 1987;

In the field of psychoanalysis there are several research narratives on the topic of 'shame.'[51] In the process it would be more lucid than has been done heretofore to distinguish who contributed to the question of the sense of shame or to the question of the sense of guilt, and who addressed both areas simultaneously or in comparison. The last topic of the list applies to the least number of researchers.

What should still be mentioned is the viewpoint that sees shame as well as guilt feelings as a subcategory of guilt. This viewpoint turns guilt and guilt feelings into a type of self-punishment. In recent times this has repeatedly been defended, in Evangelical circles by S. Bruce Narramore,[52] for instance, and by the theological Bruce J. Nicholls.[53] Narramore sees in shame the loss of self-confidence and with it a function of the guilty conscience.

Similar stances continue to be brought forward. Thus one finds that psychologists Till Bastian and Micha Hilgers have the notions that shame is the normal precursor of guilt among children and that a sense of guilt can only develop out of a feeling of shame.[54] "Guilt has shame as its precondition."[55]

---

Donald L. Nathanson. *Shame and Pride: Affect, Sex, and the Birth of the Self.* New York: Norton, 1992; Günter H. Seidler. *Der Blick der Anderen: Eine Analyse der Scham.* Stuttgart: Verlag Internationale Psychoanalyse, 1995[1]; Stuttgart: Klett-Cotta, 2001[2]; Leon Wurmser. *Die Flucht vor dem Gewissen.* Heidelberg: Springer, 1987; Leon Wurmser. *The Mask of Shame.* Baltimore: Johns Hopkins University Press, 1981; Leon Wurmser. *Die Maske der Scham.* Heidelberg: Springer, 1990[1]; 1993[2]; 1998[3]; Charles Mariauzouls. "Psychophysiologie von Scham und Erröten." München: Dissertation, 1996.

50  June Price Tangney, Kurt W. Fischer (ed.). *Self-conscious Emotions: The Psychology of Shame, Guilt, Embarrassment, and Pride.* New York: Guilford Press, 1995: Comp. also the articles of leading psychologists in the anthology from the viewpoint of different fields: Rolf Kühn, Michael Raub. Michael Titze (eds.). *Scham – ein menschliches Gefühl: Kulturelle, psychologische und philosophische Perspektiven.* Köln: Westdeutscher Verlag, 1997.

51  Z. B. Leon Wurmser. *Die Maske der Scham. op. cit.*, and Günter H. Seidler. *Der Blick der Anderen.* 2001[2]. In part. pp. 114-125, as well as the comprehensive literature list in the newest editions.

52  S. Bruce Narramore. *No Condemnation: Rethinking Guilt Motivation in Counseling, Preaching, and Parenting.* Grand Rapids (MI): Zondervan, 1984, in ist entirety, but in part. pp. 26-33 with reference to Helen B. Lewis et al. *Shame and Guilt in Neurosis.* New York: International Universities Press, 1971.

53  Bruce J. Nicholls. "The Role of Shame and Guilt in a Theology of Cross-Cultural Mission." *Evangelical Review of Theology* 25 (2001) 3: 231-241.

54  Till Bastian, Micha Hilgers. "Scham als Teil des Minderwertigkeitsgefühl – und die fehlende Theorie der Affekte." *Internationale Zeitschrift für Individualpsycho-*

## 3. On the history of Differentiating between Shame and Guilt Orientations 27

Admittedly, in linguistic usage *guilt* often has a double meaning, namely as guilt when it is the consequence of an act, and guilt in the sense of the act itself. If one assumes that sin triggers guilt and shame, then one should not be surprised how closely the two are related to each other.

### Cognitive Psychology

Next to psychoanalysis, one more representative of the less speculative cognitive psychology should be presented, namely Michael Lewis' book *Shame*.[56] Wiher highly prizes Michael Lewis and summarizes his thoughts well (*Wiher, Shame* 75-82; comp. 100-103 and often – see index 512).

### Sociology

For a complete survey of the history of research, one would have to draw upon sociology, which in particular in Lomen's and Wiher's works is practically absent.[57] At the same time as Freud, Georg Simmel investigated for the first time the sociological meaning of shame.[58] In particular, the relationship between nakedness and shame played a central role in Norbert Elias' theory. The same relationship played a central role in the civilization theory of his counterpart, Hans Peter Duerr.[59] A classical sociological presentation on shame was presented in 1991 by Sighard Neckel, in which he also discussed the distinction between shame and guilt orientations.[60] In addition to sociology, one could also mention educational science and law along with Wiher.

---

 *logie 16* (1991): 102-110, in part. pp. 108-109; Till Bastian, Micha Hilgers. "Kain – Die Trennung von Scham und Schuld" using the example of Genesis." *Psyche 44* (1990): 1100-1112, in part. pp. 1107-1108.
[55] *Bastian and Hilgers*, p. 1108.
[56] Michael Lewis. Scham: *Annäherung an ein Tabu*. Kabel, Hamburg, 1993.
[57] Comp. the overview by Ulrich Mack. "Die Bedeutung der Scham in der Seelsorge: Scham – die Nachseite der Liebe." Dissertation – Theologie: Bonn, 2002. pp. 12-20+27-34.
[58] Georg Simmel. "Zur Psychologie der Scham" (Original 1910). pp. 14-150 in: *ders. Schriften zur Soziologie: Eine Auswahl*. Ed. von Heinz-Jürgen Dahme and Klaus Christian Köhnke. Frankfurt: Suhrkamp, 1992.
[59] For example Norbert Elias. *Über den Prozess der Zivilisation. Bd. 1*. Frankfurt: Suhrkamp, 1981; Bd. 2., 1982; Hans Peter Duerr. *Nacktheit und Scham: Der Mythos vom Zivilisationsprozess. Bd. 1*. Suhrkamp: Frankfurt, 1988¹; 1988²; Hans Peter Duerr. *Nacktheit und Scham. Bd. 2*. Suhrkamp: Frankfurt, 1990.
[60] Sighard Neckel. *Status und Scham: Zur symbolischen Reproduktion sozialer Ungleichheit. Theorie und Gesellschaft 21*. Frankfurt: Campus, 1991.

## Missiology

Subsequent to cultural anthropology and psychology, Evangelical missiology, within the framework of its own specialized area of elenctics, has also become engaged in the topic of shame and guilt orientation.[61] Above all David J. Hesselgrave,[62] Klaus W. Müller,[63] and Robert J. Priest[64] are to be named here: In all cases they are prior missionaries who have Evangelical professorships. The books discussed in this essay by Lomen and Wiher also belong here, whereby, among others, a closer examination into biblical issues can be found. A comparable occupation with this topic from the standpoint of non-Evangelical missiology has not taken place.

In the process there are three schools to mention. The first school understands the Christian gospel to be guilt-oriented and pursues the question of how one can convey the gospel to shame-oriented cultures (Hesselgrave, Müller). The second school assumes that within the Bible the orientation towards shame is approximately equivalent to the orientation towards guilt, The upshot is that in every culture one can utilize a point of contact, and in the long run a balance can be taught (Lomen, Wiher). The third school assumes that in the Bible the orientation towards shame by far prevails, such that an orientation towards guilt is a misrepresentation of the biblical message (Muller, Noble, Loewen).

---

[61] Comp. the history of research in *Wiher, Shame* 132-160. Many of the early authors named by Lomen und Wiher have albeit only concerned themselves with elenctic efforts and not with the question of shame and guilt orientation and their placement theologically.

[62] David J. Hesselgrave. *Communicating Christ Cross-Culturally: An Introduction to Missionary Communication*. Grand Rapids (MI): Zondervan, 1978$^1$. Pp. 428-429+442.

[63] Klaus W. Müller. "Elenktik: Die Lehre vom scham- und schuldorientierten Gewissen". *Evangelikale Missiologie 12* (1996): 98-110; Klaus W. Müller. "Elenktik: Gewissen im Kontext." pp. 416-451 in: Hans Kasdorf, Klaus W. Müller (ed.). *Bilanz und Plan: Mission an der Schwelle zum Dritten Jahrtausend. Festschrift für George W. Peters zu seinem achtzigsten Geburtstag*. Bad Liebenzell: Verlag der Liebenzeller Mission, 1988; Klaus W. Müller. "Gewissen: Wertezerfall in Gesellschaft und Gemeinde." *Dennoch 2/2002*: 44-47; Klaus W. Müller. "Entwicklung und Funktionsablauf des schuldorientierten Gewissens". pp. 264-290 in: Klaus W. Müller (ed.). *Mission in fremden Kulturen: Festschrift für Lothar Käser*. Edition afem – edition academics 15. Nürnberg: VTR, 2004.

[64] Robert J. Priest. "Cultural Anthropology, Sin and the Missionary." pp. 85-105 in: D. A. Carson und John D. Woodbridge (ed.). *God and Culture: Essays in honor of Carl F. Henry*. Grand Rapids (MI): Wm. B. Eerdmans, 1993; Robert J. Priest. "Missionary Elenctics: Conscience and Culture." *Missiology: An International Review 22* (1994) 3: 291-315.

## 3. On the history of Differentiating between Shame and Guilt Orientations

The cultural anthropological importance of these Evangelical-missiological investigations is enormous. The exegetical or systematic theological component among Anglo-Saxon authors is mostly rather slight, for which reason Wiher's and Lomen's redress is welcome. The question of whether the Christian message and ethic are themselves oriented towards shame or guilt is not something that can only be argued from a standpoint of mission and practicality. Rather, exegesis, hermeneutics, dogmatics, and ethics also have to be considered.

**Theology and Ethics**

Theology has largely neglected the topics of shame and guilt orientation. Via mostly unexpressed or only hinted at comparisons of western culture with other cultures – for instance comparisons to ancient Greek culture, Japanese culture, or Islamic culture– theology, from the beginning onward, has actually been challenged to clarify the question of the degree to which western culture is a guilt-oriented culture and if so, whether this can be traced back to Christian influence or not.

The theological discipline of ethics should have long since had the task of clarifying the role shame and guilt play in Christian ethics and the relationship that shame and guilt have with respect to each other. In my opinion, within the framework of the theologically prominent and much discussed teaching on conscience, both sides appear repeatedly. However, the background psychological and ethnological points of view, as they apply to shame and guilt orientation, are nowhere fundamentally addressed.

Responsibility does not solely lie on what can be said to be reluctance on the part of theology to get involved in the question of missions. The same can be said about the decreasing fixation on western Christianity. The question of shame and guilt comes to theology from the halls of psychoanalysis and psychology, and in recent decades theology has very intensively attempted to make a theological evaluation and classification of almost all psychoanalytic and psychological issues. These topics have to be taken up, at least in the areas of counseling and psychology. The particular reason is that since the guilt question within the Christian faith has been so heavily weighted, a theological classification of psychological and psychoanalytic knowledge about the feeling of shame would be somehow or other both important and helpful.

Things look better in the exegetical area, even if in the final event the situation is hardly satisfactory. In 1972 a dissertation by Martin Klopfenstein appeared with the title "Shame and Disgrace according to the Old

Testament."[65] Julian Pitt-Rivers released essays in 1977 which sought to explain Old Testament incidents against the background of shame and honor in the Mediterranean world.[66] Most recently there have been quite a number of investigations on the topic of shame and honor in books of the Old Testament.[67] However, as far as the questions we are posing, they are mostly only partly suitable since they do not incorporate the question of guilt and honor. Gary Stansell traces the meaning of shame and honor in the narratives relating to David's family.[68] Whether shame here, for instance regarding incest between brother and sister, means what we nowadays term shame is not made a subject of discussion.[69]

Regarding the New Testament, such investigations are primarily found to have been produced since 1981, whereby a cultural anthropological and not a systematic starting position is more apparent.[70] An exception is found in the most recent studies on New Testament books by David Arthur DeSilva,[71] which bring together a lot of material on honor and disgrace in the

---

[65] Martin A. Klopfenstein. *Scham und Schande nach dem Alten Testament: Eine begriffsgeschichtliche Untersuchung zu den hebräischen Wurzeln bôs, klm und hpr.* Theologischer Verlag: Zürich, 1972. See further below regarding his major findings.

[66] Julian Pitt-Rivers. *The Fate of Shechem or The Politics of Sex: Essays in the Anthropology of the Mediterranean.* Cambridge: Cambridge University, 1977.

[67] Z. B. Gary Stansell. "Honor and Shame in the David Narratives." pp. 94-114 in: Frank Crüsemann et. al. (ed.). *Was ist der Mensch ...? Beiträge zur Anthropologie des Alten Testaments. Hans-Walter Wolff zum 80. Geburtstag.* München: Chr. Kaiser Verlag, 1989 [reprint in *Semeia* 68 (1994): 55-79]; Timothy S. Laniak. *Shame and Honor in the Book of Esther. SBL Dissertation Series 165.* Atlanta (GA, USA): Scholars Press, 1998; J. Cheryl Exum, Stephen D. Moore. *Biblical studies, cultural studies: The third Sheffield Colloquium.* Sheffield: Sheffield Academic Press, 1998; Ferdinand Deist. *The Material Culture of the Bible: An Introduction.* Sheffield: Sheffield Academic Press, 2000.

[68] Gary Stansell. "Honor and Shame in the David Narratives."

[69] In any case this shame was not unleashed by the fact that the incidents became known, but rather by the fact there was an infraction of Jewish law by the crown; comp. Stansell, pp. 111-114.

[70] Above all Bruce J. Manila. *The New Testament World: Insights from Cultural Anthropology.* Atlanta: John Knox, 1981; Bruce J. Manila. *Christian Origins and Cultural Anthropology: Practical Models for Biblical Interpretation.* Atlanta: John Knox, 1986; Jerome H. Neyrey (ed.). *The World of Luke-Acts: A Handbook of Social Science Models for Biblical Interpretation.* Peabody (MA): Hendrickson, 1991 (= 1993).

[71] David Arthur DeSilva. *Despising Shame: Honor Discourse and Community Maintenance in the Epistle to the Hebrews. SBL Dissertation Series 152.* Atlanta: Scholars Press., 1995; David Arthur DeSilva. *Bearing Christ's reproach: the challenge of Hebrews in an honor culture.* North Richland Hills (TX): Biblical

## 3. On the history of Differentiating between Shame and Guilt Orientations

New Testament. Mind you, DeSilva does not define shame anywhere in his overview-like complete works on the New Testament, and he only relies on a single non-scholarly journal article by Robert Karen.[72]

All in all, these, as well as practically all the investigations mentioned by Lomen und Wiher about the Old and New Testament, either use cultural anthropological knowledge about the Bible or only investigate certain aspects of the terms shame, disgrace, honor, etc. They do not at the same time look for guilt-oriented elements or array classical components of such an orientation into a larger picture – as for instance with an emphasis on the Torah. Granted, it is basically legitimate and increases our knowledge. However, it only occasionally accesses the distinction between shame and guilt, and under the systematic points of view Lomen and Wiher employ to conduct their work, it only does so sporadically as well. As a result, this literature can only render some subordinate service with respect to the basic question of whether a message founded on the Holy Scriptures has a shame or guilt orientation.

Furthermore, it is undisputed that one should know the environment of the Old and New Testaments and that this helps an individual to understand the text at hand. This also applies to the shame orientation of Mediterranean and Near Eastern societies. Therefore, Oriental conventions with respect to polygamy throw light on Old Testament events. One has to know – as we will still see – how to clearly distinguish between a description of a state of affairs at that time in history and the binding, revealed will of God. A society which starts with basically biblical-Christian values will, for that reason, raise monogamous marriage up to a personal, cultural, and legal norm. We will come back to this point and address it more thoroughly.

Prior to Lomen and Wiher the only theologians who, as far as I am aware, addressed the topic comprehensively and systematic-theologically were Lowell L. Noble[73] (Lomen 21) and C. Norman Kraus[74] (Wiher 149-153). Still, the cultural anthropological and psychological considerations are entirely in the foreground. In the case of C. Norman Kraus, who is a

---

Press,1999; David Arthur DeSilva. *The Hope of Glory: Honor Discourse and New Testament Interpretation.* Collegeville (MN, USA): Liturgical Press, 2000; Barth L. Campbell. Honor, Shame, and the Rhetoric of 1 Peter. SBL Dissertation Series 160. Atlanta: Scholars Press, 1998.

[72] David Arthur DeSilva. *The Hope of Glory.* pp. 89-93.
[73] Lowell L. Noble. *Naked and Not Ashamed: An Anthropological, Biblical, and Psychological Study of Shame.* Jackson (MI, USA): Jackson Pr., 1975.
[74] C. Norman Kraus. *Jesus Christ Our Lord: Christology from a Disciple's Perspective.* Rev. ed. Scottdale (PA, USA): Herald Press, 1987$^1$; 1990$^2$.

Mennonite systematic theologian, it has a completely different look. In his Christology, Krauss, within the framework of the meaning of the cross, goes into the question of shame and guilt and, as Wiher, assumes that the cross provides an answer to the judgment of shame and guilt.[75] However, in contrast to Wiher, Krauss ascribes more weight to shame orientation. He can do this only because in the process he completely denies the substitutionary and satisfactory atoning death of Christ and the end of the wrath of God.[76]

Indeed Ulrich Mack submitted a theological dissertation in 2002 entitled "The Meaning of Shame in pastoral Care,"[77] which worked through a lot of psychoanalytical material and offers helpful suggestions for pastoral care and counseling,[78] yet what is largely missing are exegetical, biblical-theological, and systematic-theological considerations.

---

[75] Kraus. pp. 203-228 [in part. 207]; 181.
[76] Kraus. p. 225; and against this also *Wiher, Shame*, 153.
[77] Ulrich Mack. "Die Bedeutung der Scham in der Seelsorge: Scham – die Nachseite der Liebe." Dissertation – Theologie: Bonn, 2002.
[78] Above all *Ibid.*, p. 183-193 his advice with respect to shame for pastoral counseling from the point of view of the counselor and from the point of view of the parishioner. Comp. also Christa Meves. *Plädoyer für das Schamgefühl*. Weißes Kreuz: Vellmar-Kassel, 1985.

## 4. Is the biblical message shame-oriented or guilt-oriented?

### Is western Christian theology a misguided development?

Is the massive orientation toward guilt, along with individualism in the western world, a consequence of the influence of biblical-Christian ethics on western culture, or is it a countermovement if not even apostasy? And even if a position of equal status is given to shame and guilt orientation, a question that can then be posed is: Is the guilt orientation in western society to be rejected?

Klaus W. Müller und David Hesselgrave[79] both vehemently defend the viewpoint that the biblical message is guilt-oriented, which is what Lomen and Wiher criticize somewhat cautiously (*Lomen* 85; *Wiher, Shame* 280, 136-147). Müller writes: "The forgiveness of sin occurs on the basis of awareness of guilt before God, not on the basis of a sense of shame before people."[80]

Hannes Wiher differentiates between three central axes in biblical theology: the axes of sin/salvation, guilt/justice (*Wiher, Shame* 181-188), and the axis of shame/honor (188-195). From that vantage point he sees the equal footing of orientations toward guilt and shame (in part. 280, 342). Martin Lomen assumes that the two are on an equal footing.

Other authors go much further, for example Kraus,[81] Burton, Noble, Pembroke, and Muller.[82] They consider the entirety of western individualism, the orientation towards law, and the complete dogma of the western church to be a hindrance for the biblical message. With these authors the basic negative attitudes over against occidental theology and the thought of

---

[79] E. g., David J. Hesselgrave. "Missionary Elenctics and Guilt and Shame." *Missiology: An International Review* 11 (1983) 4: 461-483, pp. 480-483.
[80] Klaus W. Müller. "Elenktik: Die Lehre vom scham- und schuldorientierten Gewissen". *op. cit.*, p. 109.
[81] C. Norman Kraus. *Jesus Christ Our Lord: Christology from a Disciple's Perspective*. Rev. ed. Scottdale (PA, USA): Herald Press, 1987¹; 1990². pp. 203-228 [in part. 207]; 181; comp. *Wiher, Shame* 149-153.
[82] Laurel Arthur Burton. "Original Sin or Original Shame." Quarterly Review 8 (1988) 4: 31-41; Lowell L. Noble. *Naked and Not Ashamed: An Anthropological, Biblical, and Psychological Study of Shame*. Jackson (MI, USA): Jackson Pr., 1975, Neil F. Pembroke. "Toward a Shame-Based Theology of Evangelism." *Journal of Psychology and Christianity 17* (1998) 1: 15-24; Roland Muller. *Honor and Shame: Unlocking the Door*. Philadelphia (PA): Xlibris Publications, 2000.

Christian society stand out. The Protestant teaching on forensic justification is a paradigm of misguided development – whereby it is overlooked that there is not a single confession in which justification – also forensic – justification does not play a central role. Its central position is not even disputed in Catholic theology. Rather, what is disputed is only its exclusivity, its classification, and the question of the degree to which it is exclusively God's issue or not, all of which does not make a difference for the question of shame or guilt orientation.

Muller thinks, for example, that in questions of salvation the issue of guilt is so central because for centuries western culture has had an excessive orientation towards guilt.[83] Evangelicals are, in his opinion, guilt-oriented, because they operate with firm guilt principles which they derive from the Bible.[84] He makes Roman law responsible for the undesirable development in western Christianity, that everything and everyone has to be subordinated to the law,[85] although he then adds – and I believe correctly so, yet confuting his own thesis – that this view was not new but rather was already shown to be the case among the Jews under Moses. Alongside this, there were too many lawyers who, such as John Calvin, had become theologians.[86] In the Reformation this led to what was called "The Legal Mode of Salvation."[87] His major objection against this is that the law is no longer valid,[88] and he poses the classic antinomian question of whether one can really assume that Old Testament law originated with God.[89]

In the case of C. Norman Kraus, in contrast, things look different. In his Christology, Krauss, within the framework of the meaning of the cross, goes into the question of shame and guilt. Kraus, as Wiher, assumes that the cross provides an answer to the judgment of shame and guilt. However, in contrast to Wiher, Krauss ascribes greater weight to shame orientation. He can do this only because in the process he completely denies the substitutionary and satisfactory atoning death of Christ and the end of the wrath of God.[90]

What surely cannot be at issue here is a lock, stock, and barrel defense or disavowal of the polymorphic face of occidental Christian history and of

---

[83] Muller. p. 18.
[84] Muller. p. 23.
[85] Muller. p. 27; similarly C. Norman Kraus. *Jesus Christ Our Lord. op. cit.*, pp. 207-208.
[86] Roland Muller. *Honor and Shame*. p. 30.
[87] Section caption, Muller. pp. 35-40.
[88] Muller. pp. 38-39.
[89] Muller. p. 39.
[90] C. Norman Kraus. *Jesus Christ Our Lord. op. cit.*, p. 225; against this *Wiher, Shame*, 153.

## 4. Is the biblical message shame-oriented or guilt-oriented?

the present time. The question, for instance, as to the degree that Roman law gave insignificant components in the occidental church too much of a one-sided impression has often been asked. I would like to demonstrate, by means of several concrete examples, the degree to which I see a danger. The danger is that the disavowal of an orientation towards guilt in western societies can also very easily lead to a situation where undisputed biblical facts are also disavowed. No more than some examples can be taken up here, since otherwise nothing less than sets of dogmatics and ethics would have to be furnished.[91]

The Christian occident has seen many undesirable developments. However, to dismiss its orientation towards guilt as completely un-Christian and unbiblical it not true to reality. Segments of culture have been shaped so intensively and for so long, not only generally by theology and the church but also by biblical convictions and standards in particular, that the danger is that a sweeping withdrawal from the present form of the western world – without checking first in detail – would also throw central biblical truths overboard.

In fact, what is even more pressing is to conform the western guilt orientation to the biblical guilt orientation and to balance the scales with a biblical shame orientation.

For instance, Laurel Arthur Burtons charges that western theology has replaced the biblical shame orientation with a guilt orientation. Augustine's teaching on original sin, which then exerted its influence on Reformers, has been made responsible for this situation.[92] He overlooks, on the one hand, that Augustine had broad exegetical reasons for his teaching on justification. Also, Burton almost seems to criticize Paul rather than Augustine. On the other hand, the motive of power and the honor/glory of God is widely witnessed to in Augustine. And of course for Augustine it is the grace of God that gives man, who otherwise lives in disgrace, a restored position before God. Augustine's sexual ethics are also – for better or for worse – strongly shaped by the aspect of shame.

---

[91] Comp. Thomas Schirrmacher. *Ethik*. 7 vols. Hamburg: RVB & Nürnberg: VTR, $2002^3$.
[92] Laurel Arthur Burton. "Original Sin or Original Shame". *Quarterly Review 8* (1988) 4: 31-41; found in Lomen 82.

**One must distinguish how one addresses the guilt-oriented or shame-oriented conscience from whether the biblical message is itself guilt-oriented or shame-oriented.**

I would first of all like to make several basic remarks on handling Old and New Testament findings.

One has to distinguish between the concern of how one makes the biblical message understandable and culturally relevant to a shame-oriented culture ("To the Jews I became like a Jew . . ." 1 Corinthians 9:19-23) and the question of whether the Bible conveys a shame-oriented and/or guilt-oriented message. The concern "To the shame-oriented I became like a shame-oriented one" (*Lomen* 16-17)[93] is surely to be agreed with one way or another, and this is not a disputed issue. After all, Lomen himself writes the following about Müller and Hesselgrave, who both are representatives of a guilt orientation within the Christian faith:

> "Both also plead for a sensitive interaction with shame-oriented people, whereby Hesselgrave, for example, considers it completely theologically responsible for evangelistic purposes to start with the topic of shame (instead of guilt)." (*Lomen* 85)

Because Christians belong to Christ alone and are solely subject to his Word, they are not only able to view their own culture and the culture of others critically. Rather, they are obliged, out of love, to adjust to others' culture. In 1 Corinthians 9:19-23 Paul substantiates the necessity of adjusting to others with the very fact that he is free with respect to everyone: "Though I am free and belong to no man, I make myself a slave to everyone, to win as many as possible. To the Jews I became like a Jew, to win the Jews. To those under the law I became like one under the law (though I myself am not under the law), so as to win those under the law. To those not having the law I became like one not having the law (though I am not free from God's law but am under Christ's law), so as to win those not having the law. To the weak I became weak, to win the weak. I have become all things to all men so that by all possible means I might save some. I do all this for the sake of the gospel, that I may share in its blessings." Apparently a Christian can also live in his own culture in a way that he does not notice that in the best case he is not understood by others and, in the worst case, due to his culture he can "hinder" (1 Corinthians 9:12) others' understanding of the Gospel. Christians are also not only responsible for stating

---

[93] Comp. also Bruce Thomas. "The Gospel for Shame Cultures." *Evangelical Missions Quarterly 30* (1994) 3: 284-290.

the message of salvation through Jesus Christ, but also for stating it in a manner that can be understood. That is also the reason why the Bible may be translated into every conceivable language and why the Gospel can and should be expressed in every cultural form.

This does not tell us – assuming we choose the Great Commission as a starting point – whether shame orientation or guilt orientation should be bolstered or corrected when instructing people in the teachings of Christ (Matthew 28:20) upon becoming Christians and being baptized (Matthew 28:18-19). However, when it comes to proclamation, what Lomen summarizes in the following applies:

> "Consequently, when speaking with someone who is guilt-oriented, more should be said about guilt, so that communication can get under way, and correspondingly the same should be done with a shame-oriented person with respect to shame and disgrace." (*Lomen* 16)[94]

## One must distinguish between what was reported Old Testament Israel and in the New Testament church from what was and is the message and will of God.

One has to agree with Lomen that the Bible was "composed, read, and handed down in a socio-cultural context . . . that features a conspicuous shame orientation," (*Lomen* 17) but according to his own statements this does not necessarily mean "that the Bible is shame-oriented" (*Lomen* 17, 28).

The Old and New Testaments do not only give a frank report about the reality of the environment in which the people of God found themselves. The Old and New Testaments also report on reality as it is among God's people. That means, however, that very often one does not find approval but rather disapproval. 1 Corinthians sketches an honest picture of the actual situation in the Corinthian church for us. And yet Pauline ethics are able to be drawn from the manner of interaction with the situation and not simply from the situation itself.

The Old Testament reports extensively, for example, on the commingling of religions in Israel, and its reports are in large stretches shaped by syncretism. In the history of Israel it was only a rare occurrence that worship of God was completely stopped in the tabernacle and in the temple. The greater danger was that next to worshiping Yahweh, the worship of gods and powers in the surrounding environment was also absorbed. These

---

[94] Under reference to Robert J. Priest. "Missionary Elenctics: Conscience and Culture." *Missiology: An International Review* 22 (1994) 3: 291-315, p. 309.

gods and powers were incorporated into everyday life as well. Any positive theological and ethical assessment of syncretism, on the other hand, is unambiguously rejected.

There is broad witness to polygamy in the Old Testament, and yet the teaching goes very strongly in the direction of a reduction in the number of wives, up to the point of presenting the ideal of monogamy. That, at least, is the way Jesus understood the Old Testament creation account.[95] In the Old Testament there are many dictatorial leaders, also among the kings of Israel. The teaching, however, sees such power in a critical light and even reports that God did not actually desire a king (1 Samuel 8:4-10).[96] Examples can be compounded at will.

For this reason one can concur with Lomen that from the entire Scriptures there is something to be learned about the question of *interaction* with a dominant shame orientation (or accordingly a guilt orientation), regardless of whether this applies missiologically for interaction with cultures or pastorally-psychologically for interaction with an individual. The question, however, of how human shame and guilt are correctly applied so that a loving and just living environment is fostered, is not hereby answered. It can only be responded to by taking a holistic look at biblical ethics as an ethic of the command to love, and likewise by taking holistic looks at reconciliation and justice as well as at the honor/glory and holiness of God.

## Biblical concepts may not simply be equated with modern concepts.

In this connection, the attempt to make the question of shame and guilt orientation in the Bible a statistical exercise relating to terms and lexical fields also has to be addressed. Such a statistical exercise is what Lomen attempts when he considers that terms for shame, honor, etc. were more frequently used in the Old Testament than those for guilt, justice, etc. (*Lomen* 83). This appraisal misses the point that the Bible also addresses things that are false and does not conceal them (along these lines the topic of adultery is more frequently addressed than is self-abandonment in marriage). Secondly, it overlooks that the frequency with which something is mentioned does not carry with it an ethical assessment (along these lines words for the lexical field for sin are more frequent than those for the lexical field for love). Thirdly, it is also doubtful whether the statistical infor-

---

[95] Comp. to polygamy Thomas Schirrmacher. *Ethik*. 7 Bde. Hamburg: RVB & Nürnberg: VTR, $2002^3$. vol. 4. pp. 771-817 and 585-636.

[96] Comp. Schirrmacher. vol. 6., p. 117-119.

## 4. Is the biblical message shame-oriented or guilt-oriented?

mation is correct. This is due to the fact that Hannes Wiher has conducted the most exhaustive survey with the aid of available exegetical works (*Wiher, Shame* 214-215) and has come to the conclusion that in the entire Bible, there are 1350 instances of the lexical field for guilt and justice, while in contrast 968 instances for the lexical field for shame and honor can be found.

By the way, it should be critically noted that I consider it problematic to simply tie the question of shame and guilt orientation to term equivalents, that is to say, to equate the German terminology found in modern psychology with German translations of Hebrew and Greek terms. Whether all instances relating to 'the glory of God' actually come under the heading of shame orientation is definitely to be scrutinized.

Terms such as 'shameful' and 'shame' often also simply have the meaning of 'secret.' Thus in Ephesians 5:12-13 one reads: "For it is shameful even to mention what the disobedient do in secret. But everything exposed by the light becomes visible, for it is light that makes everything visible." In 2 Corinthians 4:2 one finds: "Rather, we have renounced secret and shameful ways; we do not use deception, nor do we distort the word of God. On the contrary, by setting forth the truth plainly we commend ourselves to every man's conscience in the sight of God."

Specifically, the sweeping word studies undertaken by Klopfenstein have occasionally been cited as too one-sided to be evidence for saying the Old Testament has a shame orientation. In contrast, Philipp Steger offers Klopfenstein as evidence for "the 'shame' complex of phenomena being a type of legal language in the Old Testament and thus as something rooted in the normative-juridical."[97] In the end Klopfenstein writes the following, namely to recapitulate:

> "The controversial matter of whether in the Old Testament shame is coupled with guilt or not is to be answered unambiguously in the affirmative. This is demonstrated, in particular, in the roots *bos* and *klm*. All terms analyzed, however, have indeed, as we have shown, become *topoi* of legal language and namely that of prophetic forensic speech... What remains is that shame and disgrace signify guilt and in particular a subjective feeling of being ashamed, along with guilt consciousness and an implied remorse... one way or the other 'shame' and 'disgrace' are symptoms of guilt..."[98]

---

[97] Philipp Steger. "Die Scham in der griechisch-römischen Antike." pp. 57-74 in: Rolf Kühn, Michael Raub. Michael Titze (eds.). *Scham – ein menschliches Gefühl: Kulturelle, psychologische und philosophische Perspektiven.* Köln: Westdeutscher Verlag, 1997. p. 70.

[98] Martin A. Klopfenstein. *Scham und Schande nach dem Alten Testament: Eine begriffsgeschichtliche Untersuchung zu den hebräischen Wurzeln bôs, klm und hpr.*

As early as in Genesis 2:24 Klopfenstein sees "ambivalence' in the concept of shame, because "shame is (a subjective) expression of the feeling of guilt; humiliation is (an objective) expression of exposed guilt."[99] Above all, it demonstrates that often it is not being ashamed that is meant, but rather being disgraced, by which an action of judgment on the part of God is meant.[100]

All of this is not to establish that the biblical ethic is overridingly guilt-oriented. This is due to the fact that for biblical concepts we tend to consider guilt-oriented, there is of course a natural correspondence that is recognizable. This is how western culture often makes a one-sided connection between 'righteousness' and a guilt orientation. When one considers, however, that 'righteousness' often stands for God's covenantal faithfulness, it is visible that the term is also strongly shaped by aspects of honor/glory and relationship.

---

Theologischer Verlag: Zürich, 1972. p. 208; similarly pp. 33, 36, 86, 121, 137, 160.

[99] Klopfenstein. p. 33.
[100] Klopfenstein. pp. 86, 106, 158, 160.

## 5. Theses regarding the complementarity between shame and guilt orientations in the holy scriptures

Preliminary remark: Since each guilt-oriented culture contains elements of a shame-oriented culture and vice versa, and a strict separation of the two orientations is impossible, one has to speak about 'an orientation' and not in an absolute sense with respect to shame and guilt cultures.

### Guilt and feelings of guilt have to be distinguished, as do shame and feelings of shame.

In my opinion one has to distinguish more clearly between feelings of guilt and actual guilt, and feelings of shame and actual shame, than is most often done (see, for example, *Wiher, Shame*, 100). Even if this is more difficult for psychology and cultural anthropology, especially when they do not accept any predefined revelation and values as a benchmark, at least it is a central idea of theology that feelings of guilt and feelings of shame can indeed help people to recognize true sin and failings without their automatically belonging together. Thus, a person who has heaped great guilt and dishonor upon himself can be void of feelings of guilt and shame, regardless of whether he sees his sin or not. Conversely, a person can be plagued by strong feelings of guilt or shame without there being any justified cause or sin.

Nowhere in the Old or New Testament is there a situation where people have to be freed from feelings of guilt or shame. Rather, what is at issue has to do with true – objective, traceable – guilt and dishonor.[101]

---

[101] Two very good guidebooks on the topic of feelings of shame and guilt feelings are Ronald T. Potter-Efron. *Shame, Guilt and Alcoholism: Treatment Issues in Clinical Practice*. New York, London: Haworth Press, 1989; Patricia und Ronald Potter-Efron. *Schamgefühle verstehen und überwinden*. Heyne: München, 1992 (English. *Letting Go of Shame*. Minnesota (USA): Hazelden Foundation, 1989). On the topic of guilt a highly recommended guidebook is: S. Bruce Narramore. *No Condemnation: Rethinking Guilt Motivation in Counseling, Preaching, and Parenting*. Grand Rapids (MI): Zondervan, 1984; John G. McKenzie. *Guilt: Its Meaning and Significance*. New York, Nashville: Abingdon Press, 1962.

**Sin leads to guilt – sin leads to shame.**

That sin leads to guilt is so self-evident in western theology that I do not find it necessary to cite any individual biblical passages.

Sin does not only lead to guilt but also to shame. This is made immediately obvious in many passages that speak of evil deeds and conclude that there is the necessity for or fact of embarrassment or shame. Several examples should suffice.

---

**Disgrace as a Consequence of Sin**

Jeremiah 6:15 (equivalent 8:12): "Are they ashamed of their loathsome conduct? No, they have no shame at all; they do not even know how to blush."

Jeremiah 3:25: "Let us lie down in our shame, and let our disgrace cover us. We have sinned against the Lord our God, both we and our fathers; from our youth till this day we have not obeyed the Lord our God."

Ezra 9:6: " ... O my God, I am too ashamed and disgraced to lift up my face to you, my God, because our sins are higher than our heads and our guilt has reached to the heavens."

Ezekiel 36:31-33: "'Then you will remember your evil ways and wicked deeds, and you will loathe yourselves for your sins and detestable practices. I want you to know that I am not doing this for your sake,' declares the Sovereign Lord. 'Be ashamed and disgraced for your conduct, O house of Israel!' This is what the Sovereign Lord says: 'On the day I cleanse you from all your sins, I will resettle your towns, and the ruins will be rebuilt.'"

Daniel 9:8: "O LORD, we and our kings, our princes and our fathers are covered with shame because we have sinned against you."

Röm 6,20-21: "When you were slaves to sin, you were free from the control of righteousness. What benefit did you reap at that time from the things you are now ashamed of? Those things result in death!"

---

Sin is anyway more frequently denoted as disgrace that produces shame. Thus one reads in Proverbs 14:34: "Righteousness exalts a nation, but sin is a disgrace to any people." And in Jeremiah 3:25 one finds the following: "Let us lie down in our shame, and let our disgrace cover us. We have

## 5. The complementarity between shame and guilt ... in the holy scriptures

sinned against the Lord our God, both we and our fathers; from our youth till this day we have not obeyed the Lord our God". Shame is a more self-evident component of the reaction to sin, but sin itself is objectively defined as unrighteousness or as a violation of the law, respectively.

The report of the fall (*Lomen* 117-156; comp. *Wiher, Shame* 275-276[102]) also naturally belongs here. Adam and Eve's shame about their nakedness and man's hiding from God is produced through the objective infringement of God's commands, whereby violating a command was an expression of a more basic attitude of unbelief towards God.[103] Mankind lost his honor/glory and his dignity. However, this was done objectively and not only in the view of others.

Forgiveness not only ends guilt, which is a message that western theology took from the Holy Scriptures. Forgiveness also ends shame. Since the first is common knowledge within western theology, some examples should again be cited for the second.

---

**Forgiveness ends Disgrace**

Isaiah 54:4: "Do not be afraid; you will not suffer shame. Do not fear disgrace; you will not be humiliated. You will forget the shame of your youth and remember no more the reproach of your widowhood."

Zephaniah 3:11-12: "On that day you will not be put to shame for all the wrongs you have done to me, because I will remove from this city those who rejoice in their pride. Never again will you be haughty on my holy hill. But I will leave within you the meek and humble, who trust in the name of the Lord."

Ezekiel 16:63: "'Then, when I make atonement for you for all you have done, you will remember and be ashamed and never again open your mouth because of your humiliation,' declares the Sovereign Lord."

---

[102] Comp. similar thoughts on the fall of man by secular psychoanalysts, e.g., Mario Jacoby. *Scham–Angst und Selbstwertgefühl: Ihre Bedeutung in der Psychotherapie.* Walter-Verlag: Olten (CH)/Freiburg, 1991. pp. 39-45.

[103] Comp. similarly Martin A. Klopfenstein. *Scham und Schande nach dem Alten Testament. op. cit.*, pp. 31-33 on Genesis 2:25.

## Guilt and shame have to orient themselves towards what God's Word considers to be sin, righteousness, and peace.

God is desecrated when his law is violated: "You who brag about the law, do you dishonor God by breaking the law?" (Romans 2:23). In the Old and New Testaments embarrassment and disgrace are generally and repeatedly presented as consequences of sin, while forgiveness of sin puts an end to disgrace.

As a violation of the law of God, sin against God leads to guilt before God. And as an encroachment on the honor/glory of God, sin leads to shame before God. Only through God's righteousness and God's honor/glory is it possible for man's righteousness and honor to be restored. In this way, the law that defines what God views in detail as violations of his ordinances is what produces the sense of guilt and of shame.

By the way, it is to be underscored with Wiher that the situational ethic that one comes across in the Bible points in the direction of a shame orientation (*Wiher, Shame* 335-338), and that the Old and New Testaments have a comprehensive situational ethic – for instance in the book of Proverbs – embedded in the basic revelational ethic of the law.[104]

## The primacy of God's glory makes it impossible to factor out aspects of honor and dishonor from Christian dogmatics and ethics!

The Bible is full of calls to give God the honor and glory to which he is entitled (e.g., 1 Chronicles 16:28; Psalm 3:4; 19:2; Luke 12:14). At the same time, 'to give glory' is in the final sense simply 'veneration,' that is to say, worship. For that reason, it is something to which only God is entitled: "I will proclaim the name of the Lord. Oh, praise the greatness of our God!" (Deuteronomy 32:3).

However, it is very clear at this point that the biblical question is not whether we are shame-oriented or guilt-oriented, but rather how our honor/glory and righteousness are oriented. Whoever aligns his or her glory with people as the final standard, errs as much as someone who orients his righteousness towards people as the final benchmark.

Interestingly enough, what is found here is to a certain extent the biblical complementarity between shame orientation and guilt orientation in the

---

[104] Comp. comprehensively Thomas Schirrmacher. *Führen in ethischer Verantwortung: Die drei Seiten jeder Entscheidung*. Gießen: Brunnen Verlag, 2002 and by the same author. *Ethik*. 7 vols. Hamburg: RVB & Nürnberg: VTR, 2002². vol. 3.

## 5. The complementarity between shame and guilt ... in the holy scriptures

major confessions of the Reformation. The Lutheran discovery was primarily that righteousness may not be oriented towards mankind, and that in the final event it cannot be created by man. Rather, it is a gift from God. However, the Reformers – without giving up on Luther's discovery – called for orienting everything towards the glory and majesty of God and making this the highest goal in life. Mankind can just as little create this glory out of himself as he can righteousness. Through God's righteousness man is able to become righteous and come to God, and through God's honor/glory and splendor man is able to attain to the derived glory of being a child of God. Together, both lead to our being able to have fellowship and peace with God (Romans 5:1).

The honor and glory of God means simply, on the one hand, to give up an orientation toward one's own glory and not to orient oneself towards whether one is honored or glorified by other people. Shame is something an individual is to primarily have before God and not with respect to people. For this reason people are criticized who do the right thing out of fear of other people. The Christian should orient himself towards God and not towards shame with respect to other people: "However, if you suffer as a Christian, do not be ashamed, but praise God that you bear that name" (1 Peter 4:16). A life principle should not be: "What will others think?"

Many of the religious leaders of Israel knew that Jesus was the Messiah, the Savior. However, this fact was not so important to them that they were willing to jeopardize their recognition among men for it. "Yet at the same time many even among the leaders believed in him. But because of the Pharisees they would not confess their faith for fear they would be put out of the synagogue; for they loved praise from men more than praise from God." (John 12: 42-43). What is at issue is a basic decision: Is God's glory more important or is it the honor of man? Is it more important what people think about me here and now? Or is it more important what God secretly thinks and will make evident at a later time. For many Jews what took the top position was fear of the Pharisees and fear of human contempt. They feared being barred from the synagogue, which was their religious home. However, Jesus requires more than assent in secret. He wants true conversion, a true rejection of wrong behavior and affectation as well as heeding the call to turn oneself to the one true God, whom we should fear and glorify.

For that reason the New Testament repeatedly and expressly condemns 'embarassment' as retreating before men. "If anyone is ashamed of me and my words in this adulterous and sinful generation, the Son of Man will be ashamed of him when he comes in his Father's glory ... " (Mark 8:38, equivalent Luke 9:26). Thus Paul writes in Romans 1:16 and in 2 Timothy

1:8 that he is not ashamed of the Gospel, since what the Gospel has to do with is the power of God. He adds the following in 2 Timothy 1:12: "That is why I am suffering as I am. Yet I am not ashamed, because I know whom I have believed . . ." Paul was effective ". . . through glory and dishonor . . .", that is to say, independent of whether that which he did in God's name was honored or dishonored.

Aside from that, God's glory and honor is also testified to (Joshua 7:19), so that individuals openly confess and do not conceal their guilt. Regardless of an ever so impressive appearance, sin does not bring glory to God. Thus it was that the temple priest confronted King Uzziah, who wished to perform a large sacrifice upon the altar of incense, and said the following words: "Leave the sanctuary, for you have been unfaithful; and you will not be honored by the Lord God" (2 Chronicles 26:18).

As centrally evident as I find this entire topic to be for the idea that a shame orientation is a part of our humanity, to that degree I find that what is missing in quite a number of missiological publications is this pointed emphasis on the proclamation of the Gospel in shame-oriented cultures: Before whom am I ultimately ashamed, before God or before men? And who is it who in the final event is able to restore my honor, God or man?

## No self-salvation means righteousness and honor/glory cannot be produced by men themselves.

Self-salvation, depending on cultural orientation, can thus be expressed as a person's believing that he or she is capable of achieving the required righteousness before God, just as much as it can mean that a person believes himself or herself able to achieve honor and glory before God on one's own.

A very good example is Lomen's allusion to earning honor and glory:

> At least personal glory is something that does not simply fall into a person's lap. Rather, it is what an individual in a certain sense has to earn. This could in part explain the connection between an orientation towards shame and self-salvation, which was observed by Käser (1997, 165): "It seems to be that there is a form of religion that belongs to a shame-oriented society, one in which *self-salvation* is a central concern of theology" (Lomen 70).

The only thing is that self-salvation has become a problem in guilt-oriented western culture in a completely different way. This should be directed at those who want to keep a guilt orientation completely out of the Christian faith. Lomen, in contrast, wants to hold onto the thought of guilt as a biblical notion:

> "With guilt it is the act and its consequences, as already described, that stand in the foreground. In order to extinguish guilt, either the consequences have to be absorbed and / or forgiveness has to occur. With guilt the overriding point is that a person sees his guilt and confesses it. What happens after that is that the person pays, or is punished, for the guilt, and / or receives forgiveness. Important concepts are atonement, conviction, redemption, but also forgiveness . . ." (Lomen 50-51).

This, however, is precisely a classic description of Old Testament Judaism and of New Testament Christianity that would at least be shared with all large denominations or confessions, including the orthodox churches that exist in rather shame-oriented cultures. Whoever places that into question has to first and foremost systematically formulate a different plan of salvation and explain how this relates to exegetical findings (for instance to Psalm 51 or to the book of Romans).

Something similar applies to large blocks of Christian dogmatics and ethics. On the basis of the major importance of the Torah in the Old Testament, but also based on the central importance of the topic of law in Pauline theology and in the Gospels, no Christian ethic can be formulated without clarifying the multilayered question of the law both exegetically and dogmatically. The complex of themes appears among almost all authors who consider guilt orientation to be unbiblical or in the best case marginal. Their view of the law is mostly conjecture but nowhere formulated, much less justified.

With respect to the teaching on justification there is no turning back, and what may not be allowed is a situation where other aspects of the Holy Scripture receive a drubbing. What is at stake is "the whole will of God" (Acts 20:27), and this encompasses more than just the restoration of righteousness through justification.

## The Mediator is the Judge.

In addition to honor and glory, we want to next choose the concept of mediator and biblical covenantal thinking as examples. Lomen's appeal that Christ is a 'mediator' and that mediators are a hallmark of shame-oriented cultures, argues purely on the basis of a term. However, in my opinion this does not go far enough when it comes to how this term is understood in the New Testament. In a shame-oriented culture, the mediator has the task of arranging redemption without a loss of honor. The offender does not need to make any appearance.

Jesus Christ is surely *also* a mediator in the sense that it is found with respect to shame orientation! We ourselves are not able to appear before

God, because God or we would lose face in such a case. Not until Jesus' mediating role has taken place are we able to again appear with honor before God.

However, the New Testament office of mediator is at the same time inseparable from the substitutionary office, through which God's holy law is served and our guilt is atoned for. Before God we would die not only due to our shame but also on account of our guilt (e.g., Isaiah 6: 1-3). Christ as the innocent one represents us before God and takes guilt and dishonor upon himself.

Of central importance is also the fact that the mediator Jesus Christ is at the same time the judge of the world. This gives the entire New Testament teaching on the final judgment a massive guilt orientation. The point is that there is a final and common standard that applies, that everything hidden will then be revealed, and that objective facts will be the basis for judgment by an incorruptible judge.

None of this is placed into question by Lomen. For me it all only depends on the fact that thoughts about a mediator in the Bible already encompass shame and guilt orientations. This naturally does not prohibit first tying into thoughts of a mediator found in a shame-oriented culture, nor does it prohibit tying into thoughts of a substitute found in a guilt-oriented culture.

## Community Orientation = Shame Orientation = Covenant Orientation?

Lomen and in part Wiher (*Wiher, Shame* 197-200; comp. 201-211) – admittedly in accord with ethnology and psychology – see group consciousness to be practically one and the same with an orientation towards shame, as if guilt orientation would and could not also be a thing found in groups and institutions, and as if a guilt-oriented righteousness would not also contain a social ethic.

> "Shame orientation and group orientation are, upon closer examination, two deeply interwoven ways of life and can almost be viewed as two sides of the same coin" (Lomen 59; see also 59-68).

For instance Jerome Kagan considers shame to be something associated with small groups, while guilt is a thing of the anonymous, large city.[105] What contradicts this, however, is the fact that there can just as much be

---

[105] Jerome Kagan. *Die Natur des Kindes*. München: Piper, 1987[1]; 1987[2]; Weinheim: Beltz, 2001[3].

very guilt-oriented families as there can be shame-oriented big city dwellers. After all, the respective orientation shapes all relationships, the small ones as well as large ones. Guilt orientation, with its emphasis on law and justice, knows comprehensive arrangements of interwoven group relationships.

When Lomen writes: "Müller localizes shame, in my opinion correctly, on a 'relationship track' on account of the question of prestige, while guilt is localized more on a 'factual track' (Müller 1996, 104) (*Lomen* 43). Yet one has to immediately add that the 'factual track' most definitively contains thoughts on the manner in which people are to deal with each other in relationships.

I consider it very important here that Old and New Testament covenantal thought not simply be equated with group mentality. In particular, one sees that covenant is complementarily determined by shame and guilt orientations, as especially Wiher has clearly shown (*Wiher, Shame*, 200 and often). At this point relationship and factual tiers become one in biblical thinking. In covenant with God, basic relationships are defined by a highest judge and by his law (Torah) which stands above everything. The Ten Commandments are a covenantal document *par excellence*[106] and as such are determined by the relationship between God and his people. And yet it is a federal constitution with a judicial aspect of defined commands and prohibitions.[107]

This also, however, means the following: An individual is able to call upon the law to move against the community. Even the most powerful in the community is still subordinate to the law, just as is everyone else. An individual's position is not taken into account.[108] And yet, this basic law of the Bible does not mean that the group (the covenant community) is dissolved for the benefit of the individual. It does not foresee continual action against the group, but rather it provides the way to activate group structure (membership in a covenant).

The decisive question is locating what makes the real difference in the case of conflict: the opinion of the group or a higher law. According to Lomen shame orientation means:

> "Together with one's own identity and general opinion formation, ethics is not a private issue for the group-oriented individual. Rather, it is also determined by the group. The 'ethical' principle, which basically always remains valid, is the obligation of loyalty over against one's own group, even if

---
[106] Comp. Thomas Schirrmacher. *Ethik. op. cit.*, vol. 2. pp. 514-552.
[107] Comp. Thomas Schirrmacher. *Darf ein Christ schwören?* Hamburg: RVB, 2001.
[108] Schirrmacher. *Ethik.* vol. 3. pp. 112-140.

thereby other values have to be sacrificed. 'Morality among collectivists is more strongly contextual, and the highest value is the welfare of the group' (Triandis 1995, 77). The result of this is a behavior that in common parlance is called nepotism. In cultural anthropology it is designated 'tribalism'" (Käser 1997, 151) (*Lomen* 67).

However, what applies in the Holy Scriptures is that given the call of God, every individual is able to step out of the consensus of the community: "We must obey God rather than men" (Acts 5:29). For that reason, being a disciple of Jesus has a higher priority than parents and family (Matthew 10:35+37; 19:29; Mark 10:29; Luke 12:53; 14:26).

At this point I would like to bring in another thought: Without group orientation there is no biblical thought. The Bible nowhere views people as individual beings who could exist without being integrated into covenantal relationships such as marriage, extended family, work relationships, the community, or the state. The decisive question is again, however: Is God a part of this group, a part of this covenant, and for that reason does orientation within the larger whole mean orientation towards him? Or are individuals the final authority of the group?

While Lomen, for instance, correctly views the New Testament community as collective and as shame-oriented (Lomen 79), one has to refer to the fact that nowhere in the New Testament does the church have the task of developing its own group ethic. Rather, it is the 'Word of God' – be it the word of the Apostles and the prophets and / or in written form – that is the higher standard. In a central Pauline statement from Romans 12:2, Christians do not obtain their ethics by assimilating to the environment. Rather, they obtain their ethics through a continual, reasonable testing of what is good. Accordingly, in Romans 14-15 Paul does not want the differing notions the weak have to be stamped out by the pressure of the strong. Rather, the weak are to only change their position if this occurs via true conviction ("from faith" Romans 14:23), whereby Paul indeed offers very direct and reasonable arguments for this conviction. Jesus' church does not form the conscience of its members using pressure and adaptation, but rather it occurs on the basis of objective, higher, and reasonably traceable values. For that reason there is a lot of latitude provided for individuals with differing opinions.

It is unfortunately the case that many churches place an emphasis on exerting group pressure through feelings of guilt and shame, in which in the final event the honor of the church or the church's leadership is seen as aggrieved instead of consistently setting the primary orientation on God and his will. The goal of all church members is the glory of God, and only insofar as God's glory is involved can the honor of the church's leadership

# 5. The complementarity between shame and guilt ... in the holy scriptures

be a concern. The righteousness of the church is not even its own. Rather, it is something that it is endowed with by God.

Children should be raised by their parents and in the church neither with the words "What will people think?" nor with "Don't care at all what people think!" Rather, the question to be asked is what God thinks about our thought and action. It is not the orientation towards God's glory and righteousness that places God securely above individualism. Rather, this occurs via an obligation of the covenantal community.

## Community orientation does not automatically equate to a shame orientation.

Wilfried Härle writes in his 'Dogmatics':

> "The most important commonality between the three main Old Testament terms for 'sin' is that in all cases a *community relationship* (in particular between God and man) is presupposed. This can be in the form of a *given* or a *goal* which is *injured* by man when he sins. If 'righteousness' in the Old Testament is to be understood as community-related behavior, then 'sin' is the opposite: behavior *opposed to the community*. What stands in the foreground at the moment of sin is not the transgression of a prescribed norm or command, and also not blameworthiness. The injury to the community is, if anything, the reason for complaint rather than for a charge or accusation."[109]

Lomen's comment on this reads as follows:

> From Härle's description it is apparent that when it comes to Old Testament society, one is dealing with a shame-oriented and group-oriented society. The following three considerations speak in favor of this.
> 
> First of all it can be concluded from Härle's designation of sin as 'behavior opposed to the community,' on the basis of what is presented in *'Ethics in the shame-oriented and group-oriented society'* (3.1.5), that in the Old Testament one was surely dealing with a group-oriented society.
> 
> Secondly, the finding that sin in the Old Testament primarily 'injures (...) a community relationship' indicates that Israelites predominantly localized their misconduct on a covenantal level and not on a factual level ...
> 
> Thirdly, it is conspicuous that Härle stands in accord with Piers and Singer (1971) when he sees 'trespassing of a norm or a law' and 'blameworthiness' as being connected with each other (comp. 2.3). The decisive issue is, however, his conclusion that both of these do not stand in the foreground when it comes to the Old Testament understanding of sin. With this his in-

---

[109] Wilfried Härle. *Dogmatik*. Berlin: Walter de Gruyter, 1995[1]. p. 459; in the meantime 2002[2] (almost the same pagination) is available.

vestigation provides a further indication of the fact that in Old Testament society one is primarily dealing with a shame-oriented society" (Lomen 110).

At this point there is a false dilemma. Of course the biblical ethic is also a personal ethic, and its basic command is to love God and neighbor and not some sort of values, principles, and correctness. However, it is precisely the community-oriented life that means there are distinct rules of play to observe when interacting with each other. In the Bible, behavior that damages community is not just a subjective or feelings-oriented variable. Rather, it is prescribed by covenantal law. "If you love me, you will obey what I command" (John 14:15) is how this is presented, or similarly presented, in repeated fashion. Love is also tied to the commandments with respect to loving one's neighbor: "Let no debt remain outstanding, except the continuing debt to love one another, for he who loves his fellowman has fulfilled the law. The commandments, 'Do not commit adultery,' 'Do not murder,' 'Do not steal,' 'Do not covet,' and whatever other commandment there may be, are summed up in this one rule: 'Love your neighbor as yourself.' Love does no harm to its neighbor. Therefore, love is the fulfillment of the law" (Romans 13:8-10).[110]

Stated differently: The commandment to love means a perfect, complementary alliance between orientations of shame and guilt. The commandment to love equally targets disgrace as much as it does unrighteousness. It emphasizes the relationship just as much as law. Wherever there is talk of the commandment to love, one is dealing with the relationship between God and man and concrete regulations – if need be, verifiable before a court – that are not to be torn apart but are rather to be brought together.

Härle represents a particular dogmatic school which understands sin in a way that deviates from the time prior to the Reformation, the Reformation itself, and the classical tradition as transgression of the law. It is very doubtful whether Lomen, as an Evangelical theologian, could agree with Härle on what Härle says in detail on sin.[111] In fact, he appears to only use the quote and not Härle's theological direction. For Härle sin is namely a person's failure to embrace and accept human fear and rather the desire to rid oneself of it.[112] The fall of man is not seen as a historical fact, and the devil is not a component of the fall of man, just as it remains open to what

---

[110] Comp. in more detail the many passages in Thomas Schirrmacher. *Ethik.* vol. 1. Lektion 6.
[111] Wilfried Härle. *Dogmatik. op. cit.*, $2002^2$. pp. 456-492.
[112] In part. Härle. p. 474.

extent everything has to do with a personal variable.[113] In any case I would venture to maintain that Härle does not extol an exegetically justified Jewish-Old Testament and Jewish-New Testament concept of sin but rather presupposes a psychologically molded and 'modern' concept of sin.[114] By the way, however, the thought that human community determines what comprises sin and what does not is also foreign to Härle. Everything is determined by the relationship to the community existing with God and precisely not through a human community's guidelines.

## Individualism and collectivism

Many problems arise when one places things over against each other that God in his Word correlates with each other. This also applies to individualism and collectivism. Individualism views the individual, the single person, as the most important standard and believes that everything has to be newly aligned with the needs and wishes of the individual. This is roughly the message of political liberalism. Collectivism, on the other hand, sees community (among the church, with the state, etc.) as the most important standard and believes that all private needs are to be subordinated to the welfare of the community. This is especially clear, for instance, in communism or in the National Socialist slogan: "You are nothing. Your *Volk* [nation] is everything" ("*Du bist nichts, dein Volk ist alles*").

In the Bible this juxtaposition is overcome by a situation where neither the individual nor the society is the standard and goal of human life. Rather, these belong to the Triune God and his glory. As Calvin, for instance, established in his *magnum opus*, true self-awareness is only possible through true knowledge of God and vice versa.[115]

It is God who in his word imputes to individual personality vast importance just as much as he does to community. And indeed it is not only a free standing community, but it is community in various covenants founded by God, for instance in social coexistence and in working together in a family, in the church, at work, and in the state. The protection of the individual, as well as the protection of the community, are equally considered and regulated by God's commandments. Only by way of God's com-

---

[113] Härle. pp. 471-473+489-492.
[114] Also the notion of sin in Ulrich Mack. "Die Bedeutung der Scham in der Seelsorge." *op. cit.*, pp. 143-155 is determined purely psychologically, not exegetically or theologically systematic.
[115] 1st Book, 1st Chapter, Sections 1-3 in: Johannes Calvin. *Unterricht in der christlichen Religion: Institutio Christianae Religionis*. Neukirchener Verlag: Neukirchen, 1988⁵. pp. 1-6.

mandments are we able to know in which case which domain has the right of way.

Francis Schaeffer made it clear that overcoming the tension between the one and the many, which is a central and unresolved problem throughout the entire history of philosophy, is conclusively resolved in the Bible in the Trinity.

> "There are two problems which always exist – the need for unity and the need for diversity."[116]

Every philosophy has this problem and no philosophy has an answer.

> "But with the doctrine of the Trinity, the unity and diversity is God Himself – three Persons, yet one God. That is what the Trinity is, and nothing less than this. We must appreciate that our Christian forefathers understood this very well in A.D. 325, when they stressed the three Persons in the Trinity, as the Bible had clearly set this forth. Let us notice that to the philosophical questions which the Greeks of that time understood it is quite the contrary. The Unity and diversity problem was there, and the Christians realized that in the Trinity, as it had been taught in the Bible, they had an answer that no one else had. They did not invent the Trinity to meet the need; the Trinity was already there and it met the need. They realized that in the Trinity we have what all these people are arguing about and defining but for which they have no answer. Let us notice again that this is not the *best* answer, it is the *only* answer [Schaeffer's emphases]. Nobody else, no philosophy, has ever given us an answer for unity and diversity."[117]

Rousas Rushdoony, who like Schaeffer was a student of the Reformed apologist Cornelius Van Til, represents in his essay "The One and the Many"[118] that neither unity nor diversity represent the final instance, but rather in the Trinity both stand next to each other in equal measure. If unity is too strongly emphasized or solely emphasized, the result for Rushdoony, as in Islam, is the tendency towards force and towards the socialistic nationalization of all areas of life. If the diversity is excessively emphasized or set up as absolute, then there is the threat of anarchy.[119] Wesley A. Roberts writes the following about Van Til: "He differentiated between the eternal unity and plurality and the temporal one and many. In God unity and plura-

---

[116] Francis Schaeffer. *He is there and He is not silent.* in: The Complete Works of Francis Schaeffer. Vol. 1. Wheaton (IL): Crossways, 1991-2. p. 284.
[117] Schaeffer. p. 289.
[118] Rousas John Rushdoony. *The One and the Many: Studies in the Philosophy of Order and Ultimacy.* Thoburn Press: Fairfax (VI), 1978² (1971¹ reprint). pp. 1-20.
[119] Rushdoony. pp. 10-11.

lity are both ultimate and eternal. Unity is not sacrificed for the sake of pluarality, and plurality is not sacrificed for the sake of unity.[120]

Against this background the question of self-love found in the sentence: "love your neighbor as yourself" should be clarified. Certain individuals understand this sentence – mostly with the aid of psychological considerations – as a general order to first of all love oneself before one is able to love others. Others view every indication of self-love as the end of self-denial that Jesus called for (Matthew 16:24; Mark 8:34; Luke 9:23) and understand the "as yourself" as an admission of what is, unfortunately, an ever present egoism.[121]

If one takes into account God's commandments, one sees that both sides are correct as well as incorrect. If God has commanded us to care for ourselves and to produce joy for ourselves, then at this point no principle of self-denial is called for. If God assigns us the task of earning our livelihood or of enjoying our food, then such activity cannot be wrong for us to pursue. Where God, however, gives us the task of placing the interests of others above our own, psychological theories cannot reverse God's will. The Bible does not play off the individual and society, or one's own interests and interests of the general public, against each other. It is neither individualistic nor socialistic. It preserves the private sphere of the individual just as it equally does not exclude anyone from social responsibility.

In Matthew 7:12 Jesus' famous Golden Rule inseparably combines self-love and life lived for others: "So in everything, do to others what you would have them do to you, for this sums up the Law and the Prophets."

The Bible is able to substantiate the highest goal of humanity, namely to achieve eternal life and to live in eternal fellowship with God, in two ways. On the one hand, God is given the top priority and man subordinates himself humbly to God's will: Mankind will eternally praise God as his Lord and Savior. On the other hand, this is likewise the best thing that a person can do for himself. For that reason the Bible justifies a life lived according to the will of God without restraint with the benefit that a person will have from it in eternity. Eternal fellowship with the Triune God is the

---

[120] Wesley A. Roberts. "Cornelius Van Til." pp. 71-86 in: David F. Wells (ed.). *Dutch Reformed Theology. Reformed Theology in America*. Baker Book House: Grand Rapids (MI), 1989. p. 76.

[121] On the history of the term 'egoism' since carrying the term forward from Immanuel Kant to ethics comp. Heinz-Horst Schrey. "Egoismus." pp. 304-308 in: Gerhard Müller (ed.). *Theologische Realenzyklopädie. Bd. 9*. de Gruyter: Berlin, 1993/1982 (Study Edition). There it is aptly stated on p. 306: "That egosim as self-centeredness is a feature of modernity can count as a generally recognized axiom of the newer cultural sociology and cultural psychology."

greatest consummation of love towards God, of love towards others, and of true love of one's own life. This is paramount to the desire to make the best out of one's own life. Wilhelm Lüttgert formulated it aptly:

> "When through love towards God selfishness is driven out of the instinct of self-preservation, it becomes self-love. . . . Selfishness is not self-love. The selfish individual does not love at all, not even himself."[122]

Professional work is a good example of the dual orientation of love. Work is, namely, always at the same time work for the one working and work for others.

> "It does not go unrecognized in the New Testament that work should serve to sustain life (Ephesians 4:28; 1 Thessalonians 4:11; 2 Thessalonians 3:8 and 12). However, after this aspect is considered, the proceeds are also not only destined for the one who performs the work."[123]

The proceeds from work serve to provide sustenance for oneself as well as for others (e.g., family, the poor, the church, and the state). So the proceeds from work do not simply go to the worker. Paul writes: "Command those who are rich in this present world not to be arrogant nor to put their hope in wealth, which is so uncertain, but to put their hope in God, who richly provides us with everything for our enjoyment. Command them to do good, to be rich in good deeds, and to be generous and willing to share. In this way they will lay up treasure for themselves as a firm foundation for the coming age, so that they may take hold of the life that is truly life" (1 Timothy 6:17-19). Riches should serve one's own enjoyment here as well as serve others, whereby in heaven, doing the latter also benefits the giver himself. John Stott calls this "The biblical principle of reciprocity."[124]

At this point we have (once again) two aspects to take into account. On the one hand, work occurs for the purpose of providing for oneself. On the other hand, work serves others, be it because work is directly conducted for others (e.g., the work conducted by a bus driver), be it that the results of work conducted benefits others (e.g., a baby carriage that has been built), or be it that the working individual gives something of his wages to others (e.g., for the support of his family). These aspects may never be played off

---

[122] Wilhelm Lüttgert. *Ethik der Liebe. Beiträge zur Förderung christlicher Theologie. Reihe 2, Bd. 29*. C. Bertelsmann: Gütersloh, 1938. p. 17.

[123] Hermann Cremer. *Arbeit und Eigentum in christlicher Sicht*. Brunnen Verlag: Gießen, 1984. p. 11.

[124] John Stott. *Christsein in den Brennpunkten unserer Zeit. Bd. 3*. Francke: Marburg, 1988. pp. 38-42.

against each another. Thus a secular economist, who appears to have better understood the biblical connections better than many a Christian, has written the following:

> "The belief that in the end the happiness of others is also a benefit to oneself is something that only, with difficulty, finds its way into the human heart. However, it is the golden key of the economy, the key to peace and affluence and a precondition for progress."[125]

In his famous work entitled *Eros und Agape*,[126] Anders Nygren represented the idea that the Greeks only knew *eros* and that *eros* was to be compared with self-love. New Testament *agape* was, in contrast, something with complete reference to God and one's neighbor. Surely there is a difference between egotistical and giving love, but it does not let itself be tied to the words for 'love.'[127] The central assertion made by Nygren, "*Agape* does not know of a justified self-love,"[128] is exaggerated, as we have seen. Whoever places God above all else and loves him above everything, will not only preserve the life of others but his own as well.

Jay Adams[129] and Wolfgang Bühne[130] have represented the view that self-love is principally wrong and have primarily addressed their points against Walter Trobisch[131] and James Dobson,[132] who are of the opinion that an individual can only love if he loves himself. Thus the command to love one's neighbor contains two (love God and one's neighbor) or three commands (love God, one's neighbor, and oneself).[133]

---

[125] George Gilder. *Reichtum und Armut*. dtv: München, 1983. p. 19.
[126] Anders Nygren. *Eros und Agape: Gestaltwandlungen der christlichen Liebe*. C. Bertelsmann: Gütersloh, 1954² (originally in 2 vols. *Ibid.*, 1930¹, 1937¹).
[127] So in part. J. P. Danaher. "Love in Plato and the New Testament." *European Journal of Theology 7* (1998) 2: 119-126.
[128] Anders Nygren. *Eros und Agape*. p. 147.
[129] Jay Adams. *Ich liebe mich: Selbstverwirklichung aus biblischer Sicht*. Schulte + Gerth: Asslar, 1987.
[130] Wolfgang Bühne. *Sich selbst lieben?* EGfD: Wuppertal, 1986; comp. also the article in the journal of the same Gerrit Albers. "Selbstachtung – Die neue Reformation?" *Fest und Treu* (CLV) Nr. 91 – 3/2000: 16-20 as well as Dave Hunt et al. *Die Verführung der Christenheit*. CLV: Bielfeld, 1987. p. 199.
[131] Walter Trobisch. *Liebe dich selbst: Selbstannahme und Schwermut*. R. Brockhaus: Wuppertal, 1975¹, 1993²¹.
[132] James Dobson. *Minderwertigkeitsgefühle – eine Epidemie*. Edition Trobisch: Kehl am Rhein, 1993.
[133] In part. Jay Adams. *Ich liebe mich*. p. 72, who defends the latter.

Surely Adams' criticism of Robert Schuller's teaching is justified,[134] who from necessary self-love concludes that repentance and realization of one's own sinfulness destroys the individual, and who concludes that the Reformation was a mistake because it told people they were sinners. However, such an extreme example does not mean that a person has to hate himself. Ephesians 5:28-29 can, in my opinion, be wrongly intended.[135] One reads there: "He who loves his wife loves himself" (Ephesians 5:28b), and does not exclude thinking of oneself. Rather, it makes it clear that to love others often is the best thing for oneself. It is indeed also correct that according to 2 Timothy 3:2 people should not be "lovers of themselves,"[136] but – as we see in the interpretation of Romans 12:3-8 – it is just as wrong to overestimate oneself in terms of one's gifts as it is to underestimate oneself.

When Jesus makes a call for self-denial and thereby commands that a cross be taken up, he is not speaking about something of a psychological dimension – something like self-contempt or a lack of self-confidence – but rather, plain and simple, a readiness for martyrdom: "If anyone would come after me, he must deny himself and take up his cross and follow me. For whoever wants to save his life will lose it, but whoever loses his life for me will find it" (Matthew 16:24-25). This is due to the fact that this section comes from Jesus' first longer discourse on martyrdom in Matthew 10:16-42. The terms 'cross' and 'persecution' become practically identical![137]

Self-denial means to place God above all else both out of principal and without exception. Self-denial does not automatically mean to place every other person in the first position, since inasmuch as one subordinates oneself to God, correct interaction with other people follows.

To give one's life for others is in this world the highest form of love. Jesus taught this unambiguously: "My command is this: Love each other as I have loved you. Greater love has no one than this, that he lay down his life for his friends" (John 15:12-13). For this reason Christians' love is always oriented towards Jesus' greatest sacrifice of love on the cross: ". . . and live a life of love, just as Christ loved us and gave himself up for us as

---

[134] See Jay Adams. *Ich liebe mich: Selbstverwirklichung aus biblischer Sicht*. pp. 23-27 and often., similarly Gerrit Albers. "Selbstachtung – Die neue Reformation?".
[135] Jay Adams. *Ich liebe mich: Selbstverwirklichung aus biblischer Sicht*. p. 74.
[136] In part. Jay Adams. *Ich liebe mich: Selbstverwirklichung aus biblischer Sicht*. pp. 110.
[137] Comp. thereto in more detail Thomas Schirrmacher. *Christenverfolgung geht uns alle an: Auf dem Weg zu einer Theologie des Martyriums*. Idea-Dokumentation 15/99. Idea: Wetzlar, 1999.

a fragrant offering and sacrifice to God" (Ephesians 5:2). For that reason a husband should be ready to give up his life for his wife, which is a rejection of all notions of 'headship' on the part of the man that want to primarily see in 'headship' the husband's power to command: "Husbands, love your wives, just as Christ loved the church and gave himself up for her . . ." (Ephesians 5:25).

## Respecters of the person and human rights

It can be said that the Christian west itself has sufficient examples to show for the role the standing of a person has – born mostly out of a shame orientation. Yet neither a Christian nor any church can be absolved: The Old and New Testament message is that God does not show partiality to a person's standing. This applies in particular to politics, legal matters, and to Jesus' church, and it has strongly shaped the western world.

This basic principle is normally to be understood from the standpoint of the primacy of an orientation towards guilt and law. If one thinks in a shame-oriented manner, the same tenet can be understood differently: Glory belongs to God and not to man.

The standing of each person in the church on the basis of cultural, economic, and other factors contradicts the being of God and the Christian faith. God does not show partiality towards persons, for which reason not only the government's court system may not show partiality (Deuteronomy 1:17; 10:17-18; 16:18-20; 2 Chronicles 19:7; Proverbs 18:5; 24:23; Job 13:10; Isaiah 3:9), but rather the New Testament church rejects all partiality towards people (Colossians 3:25; Ephesians 6:9; James 2:1-12). James writes: "My brothers and sisters, as believers in our glorious Lord Jesus Christ, don't show favoritism. . . . If you really keep the royal law found in Scripture, 'Love your neighbor as yourself,' you are doing right. But if you show favoritism, you sin and are convicted by the law as lawbreakers. . . . Speak and act as those who are going to be judged by the law that gives freedom . . ." (James 2:1, 8, 9, 12).

Something to be mentioned in connection with the standing of a person is the topic of corruption. Lomen considers it an error in judgment to morally criticize shame-oriented societies on account of widespread corruption (Lomen 68). There is certainly a close connection that can be observed between everyday corruption and shame orientation (*Wiher, Shame* 359-361).[138] Still, what is missing in Lomen is the exegetical and ethical justifi-

---

[138] Com Thomas Schirrmacher. *Ethik*. vol. 5. pp. 139-145 and generally pp. 127-180; by the same author. "'Gib mir, dann zahl ich dir!': Bestechung und Korruption aus biblischer Sicht." *Neues Leben 40* (1995) 7/8 (Juli/Aug): 18-19 = Querschnitte 14

cation of how the broadly conceived condemnation of court bribery and abuse of authority anchored in the biblical concept of God is to be handled.

Is it not a consequence of Christian influence in the western world that in Protestant regions in particular, while corruption might be found under the threshold, it does not determine society's basic structure and in most cases can be brought before a court and sentence passed upon it? At the same time it is self-evident that such a opinion is to be stated without a feeling of western superiority and that an attentive regard for the errors of western culture should be retained.[139]

The rejection of partiality or favoritism towards individuals is to be understood as having to do with the equal dignity people have as created images of God and with the idea of human rights. I have elsewhere defended the thesis that the idea of human rights arises out of Judeo-Christian roots, even if this was formally received rather late by Christian ethics and the church. That individuals do not have their dignity and rights awarded by a group (family, the state, etc.), but rather that all human institutions predicate the dignity of man is precisely at the heart of thought related to human rights.

Is, however, the thought of human dignity or, for example, Christian ethicists' advocacy of the right to life of the seriously ill,[140] truly a defection from biblical values on account of inherent individualism? Should people's right to life be decided in a shame-oriented fashion in the future (many of those involved have the sense that they unnecessarily burden their relatives or society) or according to transcendent norms that are above everything else?

I consider this example to be a pattern of how knowledge about shame orientation can provide substantial assistance to Christian counselors and ethicists, and for that reason that psychological knowledge about shame should be a natural component of all relevant considerations. Shame orientation merely requires a healthy subordination to higher values.

---

(2001) 5 (Mai): 1-4; by the same author. "Bestechung und Korruption." *Nachfolge* (Stiftung Weltweite Kirche Gottes, Bonn) 4/1999: 30-31; by the same author. "Bestechung und Korruption." *Ethos* 12/1996: 48-49; Markus Flückiger. *Geschenk und Bestechung: Korruption im afrikanischen Kontext*. Edition afem – mission scripts 16. Bonn: Verlag für Kultur und Wissenschaft, 2000.

[139] See my article in the prior Note.
[140] Ulrich Eibach. *Menschenwürde an den Grenzen des Lebens: Einführung in Fragen der Bioethik aus christlicher Sicht*. Neukirchener Verlagshaus: Neukirchen, 2000; Ulrich Eibach. *Sterbehilfe – Tötung aus Mitleid: Euthanasie und ‚lebensunwertes' Leben*. R. Brockhaus: Wuppertal, 1998; Eibach; Ulrich Eibach. "Vorgeburtliche Diagnostik und Leidbewältigung? Wieviel genetische Diagnostik können wir verantworten?" *Evangelium und Wissenschaft* Nr. 33 (Apr 1988): 4-19.

The question has to be asked – and I am thankful to Hannes Wiher for this suggestion – as to whether human dignity is not the shame-oriented side of guilt-oriented human rights. In such case, then, the rather holistically-oriented human rights concept would have to be complementarily ascribed to the one-sided individualistic and legally-oriented human rights concept. Could not the reason here lie in the fact that in the fight for human rights in the west, it is more often either the dignity and honor of the opponent or of the individual involved that is lost?

## Against assimilation

"Therefore, I urge you, brothers and sisters, in view of God's mercy, to offer your bodies as living sacrifices, holy and pleasing to God—this is your spiritual act of worship. Do not conform any longer to the pattern of this world, but be transformed by the renewing of your mind. Then you will be able to test and approve what God's will is—his good, pleasing and perfect will" (Romans 12:1-2).

Paul does not desire that ethics and lifestyle be obtained through assimilation (Romans 12:2), but rather that life be brought into line with the will of God through conscious deliberation and action. The warning against conforming to the 'world' has always been taken seriously as a danger of succumbing to the *Zeitgeist*, or the spirit of the age, by pietists and Evangelicals.

What in the process is overlooked is that Paul does not warn against conforming to the world, but rather against conforming at all. God's will should not be followed as an act of conformity. It should not be done in order to avoid attracting attention and without actually knowing why one does what one does. Stated differently, a Christian lifestyle should not be attained through group pressure and conformity. Rather, it should be attained through conscious examination and development, that is to say, conviction.

Romans 14:23 is the best example at this point, since in this verse Paul cautions those who are strong that what a weak individual does not do out of faith is sin. It would have been a small thing for Paul to have seen to it that the teetotalers be put under pressure so that most of them would have either left or would have conformed. Paul places the weak under his protection, although in his teaching he leaves no doubt how God views things (Romans 14:1-15:3). What would be incorrect about the weak individuals simply giving into the pressure and doing what everyone – correctly – was doing? That they would not be doing something out of faith, out of trust towards God, out of a deep conviction in their hearts, but rather in order to keep peace and to fall into line.

That is a challenging message for many Christians, in particular Evangelical churches, in which peace is the first civic duty. Whoever dutifully conforms, does not ask too many questions, does not attract attention, and does not 'gripe' has better cards than the individual who wants to know the reasons for everything, who wants to discuss everything anew, who comes up with new ideas, and, if anything, is a 'troublemaker.' With all justified warning against church members who gripe due to envy, resentment, quarrelsomeness, obsession with career and cause trouble: These damaging characteristics are also found among the quiet ones. What is more, only troublemakers change the world and the church. Moses, Joshua, Nathan, Amos, Daniel, John (the Baptist), Jesus, Peter or Paul – to name just a few examples – were surely not 'well-behaved' and 'ordinary' contemporaries.

# 6. The Conscience Must orient itself towards God's Standard.

The conscience of man operates with both shame and guilt feelings. For this reason, the most important New Testament texts and the concept for conscience are to be addressed in the following. In the process it will become clear that there is no shame or guilt-oriented requirement for the conscience, but rather that God himself and his Word as the Creator of man and of man's conscience should be the highest standard of conscience. In the same way that honor and doing right are likewise the goals of a successful life, the human conscience beats in a shame-oriented manner within the context of honor and in a guilt-oriented manner within the context of law. The respective prevailing orientation stems from upbringing and environment. The Christian, regardless of whether he grows up in a shame-oriented manner or a guilt-oriented manner, will attempt to achieve a holistic and balanced mixture of both elements with the Word of the Creator in his hand.

In the classical Pauline passage regarding the orientation of the conscience, Romans 2:14-16, the law is for Paul the ultimate orientation of the conscience, regardless of whether the person knows it or not: "Indeed, when Gentiles, who do not have the law, do by nature things required by the law, they are a law for themselves, even though they do not have the law, since they show that the requirements of the law are written on their hearts, their consciences also bearing witness, and their thoughts now accusing, now even defending them. This will take place on the day when God will judge men's secrets through Jesus Christ, as my gospel declares" (Romans 2:14-16). Gentiles are those "who do not have the law."

Who is meant here? It is often assumed that Gentiles are meant, who in their conscience, without knowledge of the law, still know of an orientation toward their standards. Also in such case it would be self-evident for Paul that the conscience has to be oriented towards the law. I admittedly prefer this interpretation to another that has been testified to for just as long.

I assume, for instance with St. Augustine, Karl Barth, and Georg Huntemann, to name just a few, that the Gentiles are without the law (Romans 2:12). They are the nations which "do not have the law" (Romans 2:14). The Gentiles, who still act according to the law, are Gentile Christians, who by nature do not know the law but who by the Spirit of God receive it written into their hearts. Paul is also able to refer to the non-Jews who believe in Christ simply as "the Gentiles" (Romans 11:13; 15:9; more precisely 'the peoples'). In Romans 2:26 he speaks of "those who are not circumcised," and thereby only means the Gentile Christians, not all Gentiles. In the New Testament, "by nature" more frequently means as much as 'from birth onwards' (so it is in the same chapter, Romans 2:27; otherwise Romans 11:24; Galatians 2:15; Ephesians 2:3). The Gentile Christians do not have the law as a result of ancestry, as do the Jews. Still as Christians, they act according to God's law, since according to Old Testament promises (Romans 8:1-3; Hebrews 8:10; 10:16; Jeremiah 31:33; comp. Ezekiel 11:19-20; 36:26-27) the law is 'written on the heart,' indeed here even "that the requirements of the law are written on their hearts" (Roman 2:14).[141]

We can clarify the entire question about natural law with the term "conscience" (Romans 2:15). Does the conscience know divine commands by nature? Is the conscience an 'accessory' to the good, that is, as the Roman stoic Seneca (4 B.C. – 65 A.D.), who strongly influenced later Christian teaching on natural law, saw it as, "underlying 'joint knowledge' of the good that God knows"? Is there such a thing as 'natural law,' that which one calls the knowledge of God's law without knowledge of the Bible? In Romans 1:32 Paul sees in addition to the revelation of the Creator in creation certain 'natural' knowledge in man, namely that he is guilty of death. Nowhere does Paul say, however, that without God's revelation a person can know what is good and evil.

What speaks against people is not an inherent knowledge of the law but rather the fact that their thought and action is so shaped by moral decisions that they offer evidence that they are legally responsible. For this ethical character of our thought there are two passages from Romans 2 that can be invoked, even if they originally referred to Jews and Gentile Christians:

1. Every person constantly judges others: ". . . you who pass judgment on someone else, for at whatever point you judge the other, you are condemning yourself, because you who pass judgment do the same things. Now we know that God's judgment against those who do such things is based on truth. So when you, a mere man, pass judgment on them and yet do the same things, do you think you will escape God's judgment?" (Romans 2:1-3).

2. Every person has a "conscience," an "accessory" (Romans 2:15) in himself, which uninterruptedly registers and judges: ". . . their consciences

---

[141] A presentation of other opinions and a discussion of individual arguments are found in Thomas Schirrmacher. *Der Römerbrief.* 2 vols. Hamburg: RVB & Nürnberg: VTR, 2001². vol. 1. pp. 125-134.

also bearing witness, and their thoughts now accusing, now even defending them. (Romans 2:15).

The Greek word for conscience, *syneidesis*, consists of *syn* = 'with' (German *mit*) and *eidesis* = 'knowledge' (German *Wissen*) which is translated into German as Gewissen. The *Ge* is an older expression for 'with' or 'together,' as numerous older German words indicate. Since this 'accessory to knowing' is missing when it comes to an animal, an animal does not have self-awareness and cannot think about itself.[142]

Every person can only think by thinking morally, and in this vein one reads about "their thoughts now accusing, now even defending them" (Romans 2:15). Even when it comes to the simplest issues, thinking means nothing other than collecting *pro* and *contra* arguments. An individual can only speak and discuss with other people because he uninterruptedly discusses with himself and uninterruptedly makes ethical judgments!

All of this happens completely independently of which standards are at the basis of conscience and thought. The individual thinks in legal and moral categories or he does not think. Why, for instance, do advertisements try to connect products with positive values ('whoever buys this is independent, savvy, socially aware, or environmentally friendly . . .')? Because the individual himself makes decisions dependent upon lightning quick internal discussions when shopping ('that is too expensive.' 'go ahead and treat yourself,' 'but that is unhealthy,' 'don't think about it so much'), and there is always a value system at the bottom of one's actions. Whoever wants to get rid of good and evil has to first stop thinking!

The conscience is a function as is thinking, speaking, or writing. All of these functions distinguish humans from animals and are traced back to the fact that people are created in the image of God, because all these functions have their paragon in God. These functions can, however, be equally used or abused, since they function not only when they take God and his commands as the standard. Rather, they also function when they presuppose standards from false religions (comp. Romans 1:26-32). When people come to faith in Jesus Christ, those individuals' 'accessory to thought,' thinking, speaking, and writing do not stop. However, they receive a new standard which does not exist on its own.

Only in the Christian occident[143] was one able to mean for a long time that a call upon the conscience alone would suffice to remind a person of

---

[142] Comp to the German term 'Gewissen' Friso Melzer. *Das Wort in den Wörtern: Die deutsche Sprache im Lichte der Christus-Nachfolge: Ein theo-philologisches Wörterbuch.* J. C. B. Mohr: Tübingen, 1965. pp. 163-166.

[143] On the history of the term 'conscience' in Europe comp. Johannes Stelzenberger. *Syneidesis, conscientia, Gewissen: Studie zum Bedeutungswandel eines moralthe-*

God's judgment. Many of God's commands were known to people through their upbringing, and one could think that this knowledge was inherent to people. Outside of Christianized regions, this type of missionary practice never worked. Also in what used to be Christian countries, the conscience has for a long time no longer operated on the basis of Christian norms.[144]

The awareness of sin does not, however, come via a judging conscience that operates according to subjective standards. Rather, it is "through the law we become conscious of sin" (Romans 3:20). For this reason Martin Luther, in his conflict with the so-called 'antinomians,'[145] vehemently advocated the necessity of proclaiming the law of God in concrete terms and not only grace.[146]

The Catholic moral theologian Helmut Weber writes:

---

*ologischen Begriffes. Abhandlungen zur Moraltheologie.* Schöningh: Paderborn, 1961 (an excellent report on the history of the term conscience in Theology and Philosophy from the New Testament up to the 20th century); as well as: Johannes Stelzenberger. *Syneidesis im Neuen Testament. Abhandlungen zur Moraltheologie.* Schöningh: Paderborn, 1961. A Catholic moral theologian, Stelzenberger first sketches the notions on conscience in the New Testament as seen by Augustine through to Luther and up to the present. Then he demonstrates that the New Testament concept has a completely different meaning than in antiquity. In the Old Testament he sees the conscience integrated into the Hebrew word for 'heart.' In contrast he did not comment on the term 'kidney' (comp. the literature on conscience, pp. 8-9).

[144] Comp. on the discussion of conscience: Siegfried Kettling. *Das Gewissen.* Brockhaus: Wuppertal, 1985. Initially Kettling places classical interpretive models of conscience next to each other (Nietzsche, Spencer/ Durkheim, Freud, Seneca/Kant; comp. the well prepared table, p. 67). In the other chapters biblically reformed baselines are shown and five types of conscience as counseling aspects are treated. In his style Kettling often remains on a philosophical level. Comp. also Jürgen Blühdorn (ed.). *Das Gewissen in der Diskussion. Wege der Forschung XXXVII.* Wissenschaftliche Buchgesellschaft: Darmstadt, 1976 (Sammlung der wichtigsten wissenschaftlichen Aufsätze zum Gewissen; see the literature, pp. 489-505).

[145] From the Greek 'anti' = against; 'nomos' = law; that is, a teaching that is directed against the validity of law.

[146] Comp. on the antinomian dispute at Luther's time Bernhard Lohse. "Dogma und Bekenntnis in der Reformation: Von Luther bis zum Konkordienbuch". pp. 1-164: in: Bernhard et al. (ed.). *Die Lehrentwicklung im Rahmen der Konfessionalität. Handbuch der Dogmen- und Kirchengeschichte 2.* Vandenhoeck & Ruprecht: Göttingen, 1989 (1980 reprint). pp. 39-45 (with literature); on the antinomian dispute according to Luther, pp. 117-121.

## 6. The Conscience Must orient itself towards God's Standard.

> "In Protestant theology Luther's concept of conscience conspicuously lost ground as time progressed. One has come around again to an optimistic estimation of conscience; one understands it anew as an authority, with the help of which one by all means can recognize the good and the right. At the end of the last century there arose, however, . . . a return to Luther . . . ."[147]

Weber points out that the Enlightenment surely retained Luther's high estimation of conscience, however, it no longer subordinated the conscience to Christ as Luther did and, thereby, robbed it of its actual foundation.[148] "The individual is only left with responsibility to himself."[149]

The conscience is indispensible when it comes to the proclamation of the law and in order to compare one's own thinking and action with the will of God. It is initially the conscience that gives the individual his completely personal responsibility, for which reason it is unthinkable to be a person without the attribute of a conscience. In Proverbs 20:27 the following is said about this in other words: "The lamp of the Lord searches the spirit of a man; it searches out his inmost being."

If the law is not proclaimed, the conscience is not touched, or – what is exploited by psychologists either rightly or wrongly against Christianity – it is addressed at the wrong place. Only God can determine what sin against him is (e.g., 1 John 3:4). Conviction takes place on the basis of objectively evil acts and thoughts and not on the basis of what is with one person a more tender conscience and with another is a conscience that is hardly sensitive.

This is not intended to mean that turning to God is purely an act of conscience that reacts to law. Peace with God (Romans 5:1) is produced by comprehensive action taken by God. It includes a holistic love relationship with our Creator and Savior. The conscience plays an important role in it, but it is only an excerpt of the whole and can only react and examine. However, it is unable to produce anything itself.

That man does not have the divine law living in himself, does not exclude – as we have already seen – that the conscience as such is proof that man knows that he is held accountable for everything. Paul made it clear in Romans 1: 18-32 that every individual has a religion and a set of ethics that derives from it, even if he disputes it, and so he adds in Romans 2:1-16 that

---

[147] Helmut Weber. *Allgemeine Moraltheologie: Ruf und Antwort*: Styria: Graz, 1991. p. 199. (Weber presents in pp. 171-215 the view of leading psychologists, theologians, etc. and the Roman Catholic point of view.)
[148] Weber. p. 199.
[149] Weber. pp. 199-200.

man tenders evidence in everyday thinking that without ethics he cannot think and cannot exist.

As already mentioned, Wilhelm Lütgert criticized modern pietism[150] in his difficult to read but valuable work *Creation and Revelation* (*Schöpfung und Offenbarung*) for grabbing people's conscience instead of starting with creation and objective revelation in evangelization.[151] As a created being, mankind also sins objectively when his conscience does not communicate this to him. Only in the case of a conscience formed by Christianity can pietistic evangelization be successful. For that reason the conscience cannot become its own lawgiving authority.[152] The Gospel is not based on the conscience but rather upon the law.[153] The second chapter of Romans serves to convict the Jews, not to justify the Gentiles and their conscience.[154] The mark of the Christian is just that, not an evil conscience but rather a good one.[155]

Rousas J. Rushdoony assumes similarly that the influence of pietism (in the broadest sense) in Catholic and Evangelical churches since the late Middle Ages led to an ever decreasing emphasis on biblical law and earthly matters.[156] In this connection Ernst Luthardt has drawn attention to the fact that the pietistic view of the conscience prepared the way for the viewpoint taken by the Enlightenment, namely that the conscience itself is the standard.[157]

> The conscience is not what it is passed off to be in Enlightenment theology and what has since then become the common property of popular natural theology: the voice of God."[158]

The conscience is, however, not autonomous. Rather, it is 'theonomous.' It is not subject to one's own law but rather to God's law. What has already

---

[150] Comp. on the understanding of conscience in pietism Chr. Ernst Luthardt. *Geschichte der christlichen Ethik. Bd. 1: Bis zur Reformation*. Dörffling & Franke: Leipzig, 1888. pp. 310-313 and often.

[151] Wilhelm Lütgert. *Schöpfung und Offenbarung*. Brunnen: Giessen, 1984² (Bertelsmann reprint: Gütersloh, 1934¹).

[152] Lütgert. p. 278.

[153] Lütgert. p. 37.

[154] Lütgert. p. 285.

[155] Lütgert. p. 103.

[156] Rousas J. Rushdoony. *Institutes of Biblical Law*. Presbyterian & Reformed: Phillipsburgh, 1973. pp. 651+654.

[157] Chr. Ernst Luthardt. *Kompendium der theologischen Ethik*. Dörffling & Franke: Leipzig, 1921. p. 113.

[158] Emil Brunner. *Das Gebot und die Ordnungen*. Zwingli Verlag: Zürich, 1939⁴. p. 140.

## 6. The Conscience Must orient itself towards God's Standard. 69

been discussed about the fall of mankind (Genesis 3) makes the task of the conscience very bluntly clear. The conscience did not know the commands of God by 'nature.' Rather, God had to first proclaim the command. Still, after he had proclaimed it, Adam and Eve's conscience served as 'accessories' and accusers to establish the break of the command, for which reason both of them were ashamed and "hid" (Genesis 3:8) and tried to relieve their consciences by blaming others (Adam: "The woman . . ."; Eve: "The serpent . . ."; Genesis 3:12-13).

That the conscience is only allowed to listen for God's standard also has an enormously freeing significance. Only God, and otherwise no one, may bind one's conscience. For that reason the twentieth chapter of the 1647 Westminster Confession has the caption "Of Christian Liberty, and Liberty of Conscience." Article 20.2 reads as follows:

> "God alone is Lord of the conscience (James 4:12; Romans 14:4), and has left it free from the doctrines and commandments of men, which are, in anything, contrary to His Word; or beside it, in matters of faith, or worship (Acts 4:19; Acts 5:29; Matthew 23:8-10; 2 Corinthians 1:24; Matthew 15:9). So that, to believe such doctrines, or to obey such commands, out of conscience, is to betray true liberty of conscience (Colossians 2:20+22-23; Galatians 1:10; Galatians 2:4-5; 5:1): and the requiring of an implicit faith, and an absolute and blind obedience, is to destroy liberty of conscience, and reason also (Romans 10:17; 14:23; Isaiah 8:20; Acts 17:11; John 4:22; Hosea 5:11; Revelation 13:12+16-17; Jeremiah 8:9)."[159]

Through the conscience a person is never 'alone.' Rather, the individual always has an 'accessory.' This is expressed very clearly in Romans 13:5, where Paul calls upon Christians not only to obey the state if there is the danger of being discovered and punished, but also if there is no other witness at hand other than the conscience: "Therefore, it is necessary to submit to the authorities, not only because of possible punishment but also because of conscience." A famous anecdote by Charles Haddon Spurgeon expresses this well:

> "Spurgeon asked a pious housemaid how she knew that she was converted. The classic answer: 'Since I have converted I also sweep what is under the mat.'"[160]

---

[159] Quoted according to Cajus Fabricius (ed.). Corpus Confessionum: *Die Bekenntnisse der Christenheit. Bd. 18: Presbyterianismus*. Walter de Gruyter, 1937. pp. 129-130.
[160] C. H. Spurgeons *Spuren: Anekdoten – Karikaturen*. OnckenMiniBücher. Oncken Verlag: Wuppertal, 1990. p. 64.

The conscience also knows what is hidden, which is why "on the day when God will judge men's secrets through Jesus Christ" (Romans 2:16) everything will be evident. The conscience will be an accuser of the individual if a bad conscience has not been sprinkled with Christ's blood (Hebrews 10:2) and if there is no awareness that sin have been forgiven.

In order to confirm what has been said about the conscience, in the following overview all texts are presented in which the word for 'conscience' in the New Testament arises.[161] Thereafter, the Old Testament instances of 'conscience' will be addressed.

| **In the New Testament: Conscience = 'Accessory to Knowledge' (Greek *syneidesis*)** (all instances) |
|---|
| Acts 23:1: Paul before the Council: "My brothers and sisters, I have fulfilled my duty to God in all good conscience to this day." (There is a good conscience.) |
| Acts 24:16: Paul before Felix: "So I strive always to keep my conscience clear before God and man." (Conscience is an authority before God and man.) |
| Romans 2:15: About the Gentiles (Christians): ". . . since they show that the requirements of the law are written on their hearts, their consciences also bearing witness, and their thoughts now accusing, now even defending them." (The conscience is a witness and leads to an indictment in the heart (heart = the seat of thought, desire, and decision making. The thinking each person conducts contains self-accusation, without which responsibility is unthinkable.) |

---

[161] Comp. on the conscience in the New Testament *Hans-Joachim Eckstein. Der Begriff Syneidesis bei Paulus. Wissenschaftliche Untersuchungen zum Neuen Testament 2/10*. J.C.B. Mohr: Tübingen, 1983. Eckstein comes to the conclusion: *Syneidesis* is an authority that checks between given norms and actual behavior. Its function is identical in pagans and Christians. Only the standards of value differ, and in the case of Christians should correspond to the new way of thinking. (comp. for instance on Romans 9:1, *Ibid.*, p. 190). It is regrettable that the remaining New Testament is only handled in 10 pages, especially since among those pages the alleged deutero-Pauline letters (alleged letters mistakenly ascribed to Paul) come up, in which six important Pauline passages are found. The Old Testament, in contrast, is considered in a befitting manner, in particular the 'kidneys' (pp. 110-111 et al., see below), yet likewise measured according to Bible-critical theories.

## 6. The Conscience Must orient itself towards God's Standard.

Romans 9:1-2: Paul about Israel: "I speak the truth in Christ – I am not lying, my conscience confirms it in the Holy Spirit – I have great sorrow and unceasing anguish in my heart." (The conscience is only reliable via the Holy Spirit.)

Romans 13:5: Paul about the state: "Therefore, it is necessary to submit to the authorities, not only because of possible punishment but also because of conscience." (The standard in God's word is not followed solely out of fear, but rather also when one is not seen.)

1 Corinthians 8:7: Paul on eating meat offered to idols: ". . . and since their conscience is weak, it is defiled." (This has to do with the weakness of the standard which determines the conscience; the same applies to:)

1 Corinthians 8:10: "For if anyone with a weak conscience sees you who have this knowledge eating in an idol's temple, won't he be emboldened to eat what has been sacrificed to idols?"

1 Corinthians 8:12: "When you sin against your brothers and sisters in this way and wound their weak conscience, you sin against Christ."

1 Corinthians 10:25 "Eat anything sold in the meat market without raising questions of conscience . . ." (The task of the conscience is to examine. Likewise in:)

1 Corinthians 10:27: ". . . eat whatever is put before you without raising questions of conscience."

1 Corinthians 10:28-29: "But if anyone says to you, 'This has been offered in sacrifice,' then do not eat it, both for the sake of the man who told you and for conscience's sake – the other man's conscience, I mean, not yours. For why should my freedom be judged by another's conscience?" (What is addressed here is paying attention to the conscience of others. In 1 Corinthians 8-10 the participation in an observance involving idols as well as the prohibition against eating sacrificial meat is attacked. The biblical way between these two extremes knows that everything may be eaten but that one should be considerate of the 'weak.')

2 Corinthians 1:12: "Now this is our boast: Our conscience testifies that we have conducted ourselves in the world . . ." (The conscience is a witness and testifies.)

2 Corinthians 4:2: "On the contrary, by setting forth the truth plainly we commend ourselves to every man's conscience in the sight of God." (The conscience tests others. Truth is the standard, and the final authority is God.)

2 Corinthians 5:11: "Since, then, we know what it is to fear the Lord, we try to persuade men. What we are is plain to God, and I hope it is also plain to your conscience." (The conscience tests others and is what holds before God and mankind.)

1 Timothy 1:5: "The goal of this command is love, which comes from a pure heart and a good conscience and a sincere faith." (Sincere obedience can pass the test of conscience.)

1 Timothy 1:" . . . fight the good fight, holding on to faith and a good conscience. Some have rejected these . . ." (If a person as a believer has the correct standard for his conscience, in falling away from the faith he can only push it away, deaden it, etc.)

1 Timothy 3:9 about deacons: "They must keep hold of the deep truths of the faith with a clear conscience."

2 Timothy 1:3: "I thank God, whom I serve, as my forefathers did, with a clear conscience . . ." (Paul took forgiveness that seriously. As a Christian he saw himself in line with Old Testament worship of God.)

Titus 1:15: "To the pure, all things are pure, but to those who are corrupted and do not believe, nothing is pure. In fact, both their minds and consciences are corrupted." (The standard of 'reflection' as well as 'conscience' as a tester are destroyed.)

Hebrews 9:9 regarding sacrifices in the Old Testament: "This is an illustration for the present time, indicating that the gifts and sacrifices being offered were not able to clear the conscience of the worshiper."

Hebrews 10:2 regarding the repetition of sacrifices: "If it could, would they not have stopped being offered? For the worshipers would have been cleansed once for all, and would no longer have felt guilty for their sins." (". . . because the worshippers, having been once cleansed, would have had no more conscience of sins" – English Revised Version. Only Jesus can completely take away the conscience, that is, the consciousness of sin's

## 6. The Conscience Must orient itself towards God's Standard. 73

> guilt, not other sacrifices.).
>
> Hebrews 10:22 regarding being cleansed by the blood of Christ: ". . . let us draw near to God with a sincere heart in full assurance of faith, having our hearts sprinkled to cleanse us from a guilty conscience . . ."
>
> 1 Peter 2:19 regarding suffering when an individual has sinned: "For it is commendable if a man bears up under the pain of unjust suffering because he is conscious of God." (Whoever suffers and rightly has a bad conscience, does not suffer for Christ's sake, but rather for his own sake; the same applies to:)
>
> 1 Peter 3:16: ". . . keeping a clear conscience, so that those who speak maliciously against your good behavior in Christ may be ashamed of their slander."
>
> 1 Peter 3:21 ". . . and this water symbolizes baptism that now saves you also – not the removal of dirt from the body but the pledge of a good conscience toward God. It saves you by the resurrection of Jesus Christ." (Baptism is a sign of executing a covenant with God, and only for that reason is it a witness before others. The resurrection, and not baptism, saves, and it is the water of baptism which represents the court of justice. The water of baptism corresponds to the water of the flood, and the ark represents the resurrection.)

(Results of the overview:) "Conscience (Greek *syneidesis*) literally means "accessory to knowledge." It is an authority which witnesses and testifies to what a person thinks and does. This authority is a component of the image of God in us. This image of God in us distinguishes us from an animal, which cannot judge its own actions. The conscience itself does not have a standard. This always comes from outside (upbringing, conditioning, learning, world view). For this reason the conscience of a non-believer only points to the fact – yet all the more clearly – that there is good and evil and that the individual is responsible. Such an individual, however, holds a false standard, which as regards content can admittedly in part correspond to the correct conscience (e.g., in the 'Christian' occident).

When an individual comes to faith in Jesus Christ, he receives a new, absolute standard, namely the Spirit of Jesus, the gospel, both revealed in and made alive out of the Bible. The believer has to do more and more research on this standard and employ it. While upon conversion, thinking (often rendered in the Old and New Testaments with 'heart') is of course retained, the content of thought, that is to say, thoughts, have to be renewed from the ground up (Romans 12:2). In the same way the tool of 'conscience' remains after conversion, but it has to be oriented towards a new standard.[162]

In the Old Testament there is not a specific word for conscience. Since, however, several body parts and organs represented functions of the entire person in the Old Testament, we still find a great deal about the conscience.[163] The heart, for instance, is the seat of thinking, desiring, and deciding and for that reason often stands in unison with the conscience.[164] (e.g., clearly the case in 1 Samuel 24:5: "Afterward, David was conscience-stricken for having cut off a corner of his robe" ["And afterward David's heart struck him, because he had cut off a corner of Saul's robe." – English Standard Version]). For that reason John Chrysostom (354-407 A.D.) wrote:

> "That is why, when educating people, the humane ruler, from the beginning and from the outset, sets the conscience in the heart of the individual, which is his perpetual accuser . . ."[165]

The actual expression for the conscience in the Old Testament is, however, the "kidney,"[166] whereby the heart is often used in addition to the "kidney."

For this reason, testing the kidneys and stabs, etc., in the kidneys are repeatedly mentioned. In the following box all of the passages are listed which confer the meaning of 'conscience.' (Many translations place another word in the position of kidney, for instance "conscience.")

---

[162] Comp. on the role of thought in the Bible Thomas Schirrmacher. *Ethik*. 2 vols. Hänssler: Neuhausen, 1994. Vol. 1. pp. 769-800.

[163] Further information on the relationship between body parts and mankind's functions are found in the good, if in part, biblically critical book: Hans W. Wolff. *Anthropologie des Alten Testamentes*. Kaiser: München, 1977².

[164] According to Hendrik van Oyen. *Ethik des Alten Testaments*. Gütersloher Verlagshaus Gerd Mohn: Gütersloh, 1967. pp. 62-63.

[165] Johannes Chrysostomus, 'Homilien zu Genesis' 17, quoted in Alfons Heilmann (ed.). *Texte der Kirchenväter*. 5 vols. vol. 1. Kösel: München, 1963. p. 320.

[166] According to Hans W. Wolff. *Anthropologie des Alten Testaments. op. cit.*, pp. 105-106.

## 6. The Conscience Must orient itself towards God's Standard.

| **In the Old Testament: Conscience = "Kidney" (all instances)** |
|---|

(in its literal meaning "kidney" appears in connection with ritual sacrifice: Exodus 29:13+22; Leviticus 3:4+10+ 15; 4:9; 7:4; 8:16+25; 9:10+19; Deuteronomy 32:14; Isaiah 34:6)

Job 16:13: "Without pity, he pierces my kidneys." (There are pangs of conscience.)

Job 19:27: "How my heart yearns within me!" ("My reins [= kidneys] are consumed within me" – English Revised Version.)

Psalm 7:9: "O righteous God, who searches minds and hearts . . ." (". . . for the righteous God trieth the hearts and reins [= kidneys]" – English Revised Version. God is above the conscience.)

Psalm 16:7: "I will praise the Lord, who counsels me; even at night my heart instructs me." (". . . my reins [= kidneys] instruct me in the night seasons" – English Revised Version.)

Psalm 26:2: "Test me, O Lord, and try me, examine my heart and my mind . . ." (". . . try my reins [= kidneys] and my heart" – English Revised Version.)

Psalm 73:21: "When my heart was grieved and my spirit embittered . . ." (". . . and I was pricked in my reins [= kidneys] . . .")

Psalm 139:13: "For you created my inmost being; you knit me together in my mother's womb." ("For thou hast possessed my reins [= kidneys]: thou hast covered me in my mother's womb" – English Revised Version.)

Proverbs 23:15-16: "My son, if your heart is wise, then my heart will be glad; my inmost being will rejoice when your lips speak what is right." ("Yea, my reins [= kidneys] shall rejoice, when thy lips speak right things" – English Revised Version, verse 16.)

Jeremiah 11:20: "But, O Lord Almighty, you who judge righteously and test the heart and mind . . ." ("But, O Lord of hosts, that judgest righteously, that triest the reins [= kidneys] and the heart . . ." – English Revised Version.)

Jeremiah 12:2: "You are always on their lips but far from their hearts."

("... thou art near in their mouth, and far from their reins [= kidneys]" – English Revised Version.)

Jeremiah 17:10: "I the Lord search the heart and examine the mind, to reward a man according to his conduct, according to what his deeds deserve." ("I the Lord search the heart, I try the reins [= kidneys], even to give every man according to his ways, according to the fruit of his doings" – English Revised Version.)

Jeremiah 20:12 "O Lord Almighty, you who examine the righteous and probe the heart and mind . . ." ("But, O Lord of hosts, that triest the righteous, that seest the reins [= kidneys] and the heart . . ." – English Revised Version.)

Lamentations 3:13 "He pierced my heart with arrows from his quiver." ("He hath caused the shafts of his quiver to enter into my reins [= kidneys]" – English Revised Version.)

## 7. Concluding Appeal

God created us for honor and righteousness and gave us as people a conscience with its shame orientation and its guilt orientation. Both orientations significantly contribute to a successful life for the individual and for the community.

# 8. Bibliography

Ismael Abu-Saad. "Individualism and Islamic Work Beliefs." *Journal of Cross-Cultural Psychology* 29 (1998) 2: 377-383.

Franz Alexander. *Fundamentals of Psychoanalysis*. New York: Norton, 1948[1], 1963[2].

Thomas L. Austin. "Elenctics." pp. 307-308 in: A. Scott Moreau. *Evangelical Dictionary of World Missions*. Baker Book House: Grand Rapids (MI), 2000.

David P. Ausubel. "Relationships between Shame and Guilt in the Socializing Process." *Psychological Review* 62 (1955): 378-390.

David P. Ausubel. *Theory and Problems of Child Development*. New York: Grune & Stratton, 1958[1]; 1970[2]; 1980[3].

David P. Ausubel, Edmund V. Sullivan. *Das Kindesalter: Fakten, Probleme, Theorie*. München: Juventa Verlag, 1974.

David P. Ausubel. "Relationships between Shame and Guilt in the Socializing Process." *Psychological Review* 62 (1955): 378-390.

Till Bastian. *Der Blick, die Scham, das Gefühl: Eine Anthropologie des Verkannten*. Göttingen: Vandenhoeck & Ruprecht, 1998.

Till Bastian, Micha Hilgers. "Kain – Die Trennung von Scham und Schuld am Beispiel der Genesis." *Psyche* 44 (1990): 1100-1112.

Till Bastian, Micha Hilgers. "Scham als Teil des Minderwertigkeitsgefühls – und die fehlende Theorie der Affekte." *Internationale Zeitschrift für Individualpsychologie* 16 (1991): 102-110.

Ruth Benedict. *The Chrysanthenum and the Sword: Patterns of Japanese Culture*. Boston: Houghton and Mifflin, 1946.

Ruth Benedict. "Religion." pp. 627-665 in: Franz Boas (ed.). *General Anthropology. War Department Educational Manual 226*. Boston (USA): Heath/Madison (WI): US Armed Forces Inst., 1938; 1944; reprint: New York: Johnson, 1965.

Wolfgang Blankenburg. "Zur Differenzierung von Scham und Schuld". pp. 45-56 in: Rolf Kühn, Michael Raub, Michael Titze (eds.). *Scham – ein menschliches Gefühl: Kulturelle, psychologische und philosophische Perspektiven*. Köln: Westdeutscher Verlag, 1997.

Franz Boas. *Race, Language and Culture*. New York: The Macmillan Comp., 1948.

Franz Boas (ed.). *General Anthropology. War Department Educational Manual 226*. Boston (USA): Heath/Madison (WI): US Armed Forces Inst., 1938; 1944; Nachdruck: New York: Johnson, 1965.

Francis J. Broucek. *Shame and the Self*. New York: The Guilford Press, 1991.

Richard Buda, Sayed M. Elsayed-Elkhouly. "Cultural Differences between Arabs and Americans: Individualism-Collectivism Revisited." *Journal of Cross-Cultural Psychology* 29 (1998) 3: 487-492.

Laurel Arthur Burton. "Original Sin or Original Shame." *Quarterly Review* 8 (1988) 4: 31-41.

Barth L. Campbell. "Honor, Shame, and the Rhetoric of 1 Peter." *SBL Dissertation Series* 160. Atlanta: Scholars Press, 1998.

Ferdinand Deist. *The Material Culture of the Bible: An Introduction.* Sheffield: Sheffield Academic Press, 2000.
David Arthur DeSilva. "Despising Shame: Honor Discourse and Community Maintenance in the Epistle to the Hebrews." *SBL Dissertation Series* 152. Atlanta: Scholars Press, 1995
David Arthur DeSilva. *Bearing Christ's Reproach: The Challenge of Hebrews in an Honor Culture.* North Richland Hills (TX): Biblical Press, 1999.
David Arthur DeSilva. *The Hope of Glory: Honor Discourse and New Testament Interpretation.* Collegeville (USA): Liturgical Press, 2000.
Eric Robertson Dodds. *Die Griechen und das Irrationale.* Wissenschaftliche Buchgesellschaft: Darmstadt, $1970^1$; $1976^2$; reprint 1991.
Eric Robertson Dodds. *The Greeks and the Irrational.* Berkeley: Univ. of California Press, 1951; 15. printed 1984.
Hans Peter Duerr. *Nacktheit und Scham: Der Mythos vom Zivilisationsprozess. Bd. 1.* Suhrkamp: Frankfurt, $1988^1$; $1988^2$.
Hans Peter Duerr. *Nacktheit und Scham. Bd. 2.* Suhrkamp: Frankfurt, 1990.
Wolfram Eberhard. *Guilt and Sin in Traditional China.* Berkeley (USA): University of California Press, 1967.
Robert B. Edgerton. *Sick Societies: Challenging the Myth of Primitive Harmony.* The Free Press: New York, 1992.
Norbert Elias. *Über den Prozess der Zivilisation. Bd. 1.* Frankfurt: Suhrkamp, 1981.
Norbert Elias. *Über den Prozess der Zivilisation. Bd. 2.* Frankfurt: Suhrkamp, 1982.
Mario Erdheim. "Sigmund Freud (1856-1939)," pp. 137-150 in: Wolfgang Marschall (ed.). *Klassiker der Kulturanthropologie: Von Montaigne bis Margaret Mead.* München: C. H. Beck, 1990.
J. Cheryl Exum, Stephen D. Moore. *Biblical studies, cultural studies: The third Sheffield Colloquium.* Sheffield: Sheffield Academic Press, 1998.
Derek Freeman. *Liebe ohne Aggression: Margaret Meads Legende von der Friedfertigkeit der Naturvölker.* Kindler: München, 1983.
Walter Goldschmidt (ed.). *The Anthropology of Franz Boas: Essays on the Centennial of His Birth.* Washington, D.C., The American Anthropological Association, 1959.
Douglas Graham. *Moral Learning and Development.* London: Batsdorf, 1972.
Roland Girtler. *Kulturanthropologie.* dtv wissenschaft. dtv: München, 1979. pp. 34-37.
Wilfried Härle. *Dogmatik.* Berlin: Walter de Gruyter, $1995^1$; $2002^2$.
David J. Hesselgrave. "Missionary Elenctics and Guilt and Shame." *Missiology: An International Review 11* (1983) 4: 461-483.
David J. Hesselgrave, David J. *Communicating Christ Cross-Culturally: An Introduction to Missionary Communication.* Grand Rapids (MI): Zondervan, $1978^1$; $1991^2$.
Micha Hilgers. *Scham: Gesichter eines Affekts.* Göttingen: Vandenhoeck & Ruprecht, $1996^1$; $1997^2$.
Mario Jacoby. *Scham–Angst und Selbstwertgefühl: Ihre Bedeutung in der Psychotherapie.* Walter-Verlag: Olten (CH)/Freiburg, 1991.
Ronald C. Johnson et al. "Guilt, Shame and adjustment in three cultures." *Journal of Individual Differences* 8 (1987) 3: 357-364.

# 8. Bibliography

Lothar Käser. *Fremde Kulturen: Eine Einführung in die Ethnologie.* VLM: Lahr & Verlag der Evang.-Luth. Mission: Erlangen, 1998². Chapter 10. "Kultur und Über-Ich (Gewissen)," pp. 129-167.

Jerome Kagan. *Die Natur des Kindes.* München: Piper, 1987¹; 1987²; Weinheim: Beltz, 2001³.

Gershen Kaufman. *Shame: The Power of Caring.* Cambridge, MA: Schenckman. 1980¹; 1992².

Gershen Kaufman. *The Psychology of Shame: Theory and Treatment of Shame-Based Syndromes.* New York: Springer, 1989.

Gershen Kaufman, L. Raphael. "Shame: A Perspective on Jewish Identity." *Journal of Psychology and Judaism* 11 (1987): 30-40.

Ward Keeler. "Shame and Stage Fright in Java." *Ethos: Journal of the Society for Psychological Anthropology* 2 (1983) 3: 152-165.

Shinobu S. Kitayama (ed.). *Emotion and Culture: Empirical Studies of Mutual Influence.* Washington, DC: American Psychological Association Press, 1994.

Martin A. Klopfenstein. *Scham und Schande nach dem Alten Testament: Eine begriffsgeschichtliche Untersuchung zu den hebräischen Wurzeln bôs, klm und hpr.* Theologischer Verlag: Zürich, 1972.

Walter Krämer et al. *Das neue Lexikon der populären Irrtümer.* Eichborn: Frankfurt, 1998. pp. 290-291.

C. Norman Kraus. "The Cross of Christ – Dealing with Shame and Guilt". *Japan Christian Quarterly* 53 (1987): 221-227.

C. Norman Kraus. *Jesus Christ Our Lord: Christology from a Disciple's Perspective.* Rev. ed. Scottdale: Herald Press, 1987¹; 1990².

Rolf Kühn, Michael Raub. Michael Titze (ed.). *Scham – ein menschliches Gefühl: Kulturelle, psychologische und philosophische Perspektiven.* Köln: Westdeutscher Verlag, 1997.

Timothy S. Laniak. "Shame and Honor in the Book of Esther." *SBL Dissertation Series* 165. Atlanta (GE): Scholars Press, 1998.

Melvin R. Lansky, Andrew P. Morrison. "The Legacy of Freud's Writings on Shame." pp. 3-40 in: Melvin R. Lansky, Andrew P. Morrison (ed.). *The Widening Scope of Shame.* Hillsdale (NJ): The Analytic Press, 1997.

Melvin R. Lansky, Andrew P. Morrison (ed.). *The Widening Scope of Shame.* Hillsdale (NJ): The Analytic Press, 1997.

Takie Sugiyama Lebra. "On Social Mechanisms of Guilt and Shame": The Japanese case." *Anthropological Quarterly* 44 (1971): 241-245.

Takie Sugiyama Lebra. "Shame and Guilt: A Psychocultural View of the Japanese Self." *Ethos: Journal of the Society for Psychological Anthropology* 2 (1983) 3: 192-209.

Zuk-Nae Lee. "Koreanische Kultur und Schamgefühl." pp. 75-86 in: Rolf Kühn, Michael Raub. Michael Titze (eds.). *Scham – ein menschliches Gefühl: Kulturelle, psychologische und philosophische Perspektiven.* Köln: Westdeutscher Verlag, 1997.

Helen B. Lewis. *Shame and Guilt in Neurosis.* New York: International Universities Press, 1971.

Michael Lewis. *Scham: Annäherung an ein Tabu.* Hamburg: Kabel, 1993.

Ruth Lienhard. "Ehre und Recht." pp. 253-263 in: Klaus W. Müller (ed.). *Mission in fremden Kulturen: Festschrift für Lothar Käser*. edition afem – edition academics 15. Nürnberg: VTR, 2004.

Jacob Abram Loewen. *Culture and Human Values: Christian Intervention in Anthropological Perspective*. Pasadena (CA): William Carey Library, 1975 (= 1977).

Jacob Abram Loewen. *The Bible in Cross-Cultural Perspective*. Pasadena: William Carey Library, 2000.

Martin Lomen. *Sünde und Scham im biblischen und islamischen Kontext: Ein ethnohermeneutischer Beitrag zum christlich-islamischen Dialog*. Edition afem – mission scripts 21. Nürnberg: VTR, 2003.

Helen Merell Lynd. *On Shame and the Search of Identity*. London: Routledge and Kegan Paul, 1958; New York: Science Editions, 1961.

Ulrich Mack. "Die Bedeutung der Scham in der Seelsorge: Scham – die Nachseite der Liebe." Dissertation – Theologie: Bonn, 2002.

Bruce J. Manila. *The New Testament World: Insights from Cultural Anthropology*. Atlanta: John Knox, 1981.

Bruce J. Manila. *Christian Origins and Cultural Anthropology: Practical Models for Biblical Interpretation*. Atlanta: John Knox, 1986.

Charles Mariauzouls. *Psychophysiologie von Scham und Erröten*. München: Dissertation, 1996.

John G. McKenzie. *Guilt: Its Meaning and Significance*. New York, Nashville: Abingdon Press, 1962.

Margret Mead (Hg.). *Cooperation and Competition Among Primitive Peoples*. New York: McGraw-Hill Book Company, 1937; Rev. Ed. Boston: Beacon Press, 1961.

Margaret Mead. "Apprenticeship Under Boas." pp. 29-45 in: Walter Goldschmidt (ed.). *The Anthropology of Franz Boas: Essays on the Centennial of His Birth*. Washington, D.C., The American Anthropological Association, 1959.

Christa Meves. *Plädoyer für das Schamgefühl*. Weißes Kreuz: Vellmar-Kassel, 1985.

Andrew P. Morrison. *Shame: The Underside of Narcissism*. Hillsdale (NJ): The Analytic Press, 1989.

Andrew P. Morrison. *The Culture of Shame*. Northvale (NJ)/London: Jason Aronson, 1998.

Klaus W. Müller. "Elenktik: Die Lehre vom scham- und schuldorientierten Gewissen". *Evangelikale Missiologie* 12 (1996): 98-110.

Klaus W. Müller. "Elenktik: Gewissen im Kontext." pp. 416-451 in: Hans Kasdorf, Klaus W. Müller (eds.). *Bilanz und Plan: Mission an der Schwelle zum Dritten Jahrtausend. Festschrift für George W. Peters zu seinem achtzigsten Geburtstag*. Bad Liebenzell: Verlag der Liebenzeller Mission, 1988.

Klaus W. Müller. "Gewissen: Wertezerfall in Gesellschaft und Gemeinde." *Dennoch* 2/2002: 44-47.

Klaus W. Müller. "Entwicklung und Funktionsablauf des schuldorientierten Gewissens." pp. 264-290 in: Klaus W. Müller (ed.). *Mission in fremden Kulturen: Festschrift für Lothar Käser*. edition afem – edition academics 15. Nürnberg: VTR, 2004.

# 8. Bibliography

Roland Muller. *Honor and Shame: Unlocking the Door.* Philadelphia (PA): Xlibris Publications, 2000.
S. Bruce Narramore. *No Condemnation: Rethinking Guilt Motivation in Counseling, Preaching, and Parenting.* Grand Rapids (MI): Zondervan, 1984.
Donald L. Nathanson (ed.). *The Many Faces of Shame.* New York: Guilford Press, 1987.
Donald L. Nathanson. *Shame and Pride: Affect, Sex, and the Birth of the Self.* New York: Norton, 1992.
Sighard Neckel. *Status und Scham: Zur symbolischen Reproduktion sozialer Ungleichheit. Theorie und Gesellschaft* 21. Frankfurt: Campus, 1991.
Jerome H. Neyrey (ed.). *The World of Luke-Acts: A Handbook of Social Science Models for Biblical Interpretation.* Peabody (MA): Hendrickson, 1991 (= 1993).
Bruce J. Nicholls. "The Role of Shame and Guilt in a Theology of Cross-Cultural Mission." *Evangelical Review of Theology* 25 (2001) 3: 231-241.
Lowell L. Noble. *Naked and Not Ashamed: An Anthropological, Biblical, and Psychological Study of Shame.* Jackson (MI): Jackson Pr., 1975.
Neil F. Pembroke. "Toward a Shame-Based Theology of Evangelism." *Journal of Psychology and Christianity* 17 (1998) 1: 15-24.
Jean G. Peristiany (ed.). *Honor and Shame: The Values of a Mediterranean Society.* London: Weidenfeld and Nicolson, 1965; Chicago: University of Chicago, 1966 (= 1970; 1974).
John George Peristiany, Julian Pitt-Rivers (ed.). *Honour and Grace in Anthropology.* Cambridge: Cambridge University Press, 1992; Cambridge University Press – Digital Printing, 1999.
Kenneth L. Pike. "Christianity and Culture: I. Conscience and Culture." Journal of the American Scientific Affiliation 31 (1979): 8-12.
Gerhart Piers, Milton B. Singer. *Shame and Guilt: A Psychoanalytic and Cultural Study.* Springfield (IL): Charles C. Thomas, 1953; New York: Norton, 1971.
Paul Ricoeur. *Symbolik des Bösen. Phänomenologie der Schuld II.* Freiburg: Alber, 1960; 1971.
Paul Ricoeur. *Die Fehlbarkeit des Menschen. Phänomenologie der Schuld I.* Freiburg: Alber, 1960; 1971.
Julian Pitt-Rivers. *The Fate of Shechem or The Politics of Sex: Essays in the Anthropology of the Mediterranean.* Cambridge: Cambridge University, 1977.
Patricia und Ronald Potter-Efron. *Schamgefühle verstehen und überwinden.* Heyne: München, 1992 (English *Letting Go of Shame.* Minnesota (USA): Hazelden Foundation, 1989).
Ronald T. Potter-Efron. Shame, *Guilt and Alcoholism: Treatment Issues in Clinical Practice.* New York, London: Haworth Press, 1989.
Robert J. Priest. "Cultural Anthropology, Sin and the Missionary." pp. 85-105 in: D. A. Carson und John D. Woodbridge (eds.). *God and Culture: Essays in honor of Carl F. Henry.* Grand Rapids (MI): Wm. B. Eerdmans, 1993.
Robert J. Priest. Missionary *Elenctics: Conscience and Culture. Missiology: An International Review* 22 (1994) 3: 291-315.

Joseph Sandler. "Zum Begriff des Überichs." pp. 45-81 in: Karola Brede (ed.). *Das Überich und die Macht seiner Objekte: [50 Jahre Psyche]*. Stuttgart: Verlag Internationale Psychoanalyse, 1996.
Christine Schirrmacher. *Kleines Lexikon der islamischen Familie*. Holzgerlingen: Hänssler, 2002. Eintrag "Ehre und Schande", pp. 58-67.
Christine Schirrmacher. *Herausforderung Islam*. Holzgerlingen: Hänssler, 2002. Kapitel "Terroanschläge gegen den Ehrverlust", pp. 72-86.
Thomas Schirrmacher. *Ethik*. 7 vols. VTR: Nürnberg & RVB: Hamburg, 2002³.
Thomas Schirrmacher (ed.) *Die vier Schöpfungsordnungen Gottes: Kirche, Staat, Wirtschaft und Familie bei Dietrich Bonhoeffer und Martin Luther*. VTR: Nürnberg, 2001.
Thomas Schirrmacher, Christine Schirrmacher et. al. *Harenberg Lexikon der Religionen*. Harenberg Verlag: Düsseldorf, 2002.
Thomas Schirrmacher. *Führen in ethischer Verantwortung, Die drei Seiten jeder Entscheidung*. Gießen: Brunnen, 2002.
Hanna-Maria Schmalenbach. "Die Lüge als Überlebensstrategie in schamorientierten und furchtbestimmten Kulturen." Mexico Report Juni 2002: 17-23 (Kurzfassung von:)
Hanna-Maria Schmalenbach. "Die Lüge als Überlebensstrategie: Gedanken und Erfahrungen aus einer Missionsarbeit in Mexico." Unveröffentlichte Semesterarbeit. Columbia International University Deutscher Zweig, Korntal, 2001.
"Schuld/Schuldgefühle". pp. 242-247 in: *Lexikon der Bioethik*. 3 vols. vol. 3. Gütersloher Verlagshaus: Gütersloh, 1998. pp. 246-247.
Günter H. Seidler. *Der Blick der Anderen: Eine Analyse der Scham*. Stuttgart: Verlag Internationale Psychoanalyse, 1995¹; Stuttgart: Klett-Cotta, 2001².
Melford E. Spiro. *The Children of the Kibbutz: A study in child training and personality*. Cambridge (MS): Harvard University Press, 1958; Rev. edition. 1975.
Gary Stansell. "Honor and Shame in the David Narratives." pp. 94-114 in: Frank Crüsemann et. al. (ed.). *Was ist der Mensch ...? Beiträge zur Anthropologie des Alten Testaments. Hans-Walter Wolff zum 80. Geburtstag*. München: Chr. Kaiser Verlag, 1989 (reprinted as:)
Gary Stansell. "Honor and Shame in the David Narratives." Semeia 68 (1994): 55-79.
Helm Stierlin. *Adolf Hitler: Familienperspektiven*. Suhrkamp taschenbuch 2361. Frankfurt: Suhrkamp, new edition 1995 (1975).
Deborah Stipek. "Differences between Americans and Chinese in the circumstances evoking pride, shame, and guilt." *Journal of Cross-cultural Psychology* 29 (1998) 5: 616-629.
Denise L. Sweetnam. *Kurdish Culture: A Cross-Cultural Guide. Untersuchungen zur kurdischen Sprache und Kultur* 4. Bonn: VKW, 2004². pp. 59-114.
June Price Tangney, Kurt W. Fischer (ed.). *Self-conscious Emotions: The Psychology of Shame, Guilt, Embarrassment, and Pride*. New York: Guilford Press, 1995.
Bruce Thomas. "The Gospel for Shame Cultures." *Evangelical Missions Quarterly* 30 (1994) 3: 284-290.
R. L. Timpe. "Shame." pp. 1074-1075 in: David G. Benner (ed.). *Baker's Encyclopedia of Psychology*. Grand Rapids (MI): Baker Books, 1985.

# 8. Bibliography

Colin M. Turnbull. *Das Volk ohne Liebe: Der soziale Untergang der Ik.* Rowohlt: Reinbek, 1973.

Hannes Wiher. *Missionsdienst in Guinea: Das Evangelium für eine schamorientierte, von Animismus und Volksislam geprägten Gesellschaft.* edition afem, mission scripts 14. Bonn: Verlag für Kultur und Wissenschaft, 1998 (French edition:)

Hannes Wiher. *L'Évangile et la Culture de Honte en Afrique Occidentale.* edition iwg, mission scripts 21. Bonn: Verlag für Kultur und Wissenschaft, 2003.

Hannes Wiher. *Shame and Guilt: A Key to Cross-Cultural Ministry.* edition iwg – mission academics 10. Bonn: Verlag für Kultur und Wissenschaft, 2003.

Hannes Wiher. "Der Animismus als schamorientiertes System." pp. 291-305 in: Klaus W. Müller (ed.). *Mission in fremden Kulturen: Festschrift für Lothar Käser.* edition afem – edition academics 15. Nürnberg: VTR, 2004.

Leon Wurmser. *The Mask of Shame.* Baltimore: Johns Hopkins University Press, 1981.

Leon Wurmser. *The Mask of Shame.* Baltimore: Johns Hopkins University Press, 1981.

Leon Wurmser. *Die Flucht vor dem Gewissen.* Heidelberg: Springer, 1987.

# About the Author

## Books by Thomas Schirrmacher in chronological order (With short commentaries)

*For a full book list see www.thomasschirrmacher.net/eine-seite/books-published.*

### Selection from the author's books:

Theodor Christlieb und seine Missionstheologie. Verlag der Evangelischen Gesellschaft für Deutschland: Wuppertal, 1985. 308 pp.

[Theodor Christlieb and his theology of mission] *A study of the biography, theology and missiology of the leading German Pietist, professor of practical theology and international missions leader in the second half of the nineteenth century.*

Marxismus: Opium für das Volk? Schwengeler: Berneck (CH), 1990[1], 1997[2]. 150 pp.

[Marxism: Opiate for the People?] *Marxism is proven to be a religion and an opiate for the masses. Empasizes the differences between Marxist and Biblical work ethics.*

Paul in Conflict with the Veil!? VTR: Nürnberg, 2002[1]; 2007[2]. 130 pp.

*Exegetical examination of 1. Corinthians 11,2-16, following an alternative view of John Lightfoot, member of the Westminster assembly in the 16th century.*

Ethik. Neuhausen: Hänssler, 1994[1]. 2 vol. 883 & 889 pp.; Hamburg: RVB & Nürnberg: VTR, 2001[2]. 3 vol. 2150 pp.; 2002[3], 2009[4]; 2011[5]. 8 volumes. 2850 pp.

[Ethics] *Major Evangelical ethics in German covering all aspects of general, special, persocial and public ethics.*

Legends About the Galilei-Affair. RVB International: Hamburg, 2001[1]; 2008.[2]. 120 pp.

Law or Spirit? An Alternative View of Galatians. RVB International: Hamburg, 2001[1]; 2008.[2]. 160 pp.

*This commentary emphasising the ethical aspects of Galatians wants to prove that Galatians is not only fighting legalists but also a second party of Paul's opponents, who were totally opposed to the Old Testament and the Law.*

God Wants You to Learn, Labour and Love. Reformation Books: Hamburg, 1999. 120 pp.

*Four essays for Third World Christian Leaders on Learning with Jesus, Work Ethic, Love and Law and Social Involvement.*

World Mission – Heart of Christianity. RVB International: Hamburg, 1999[1]; 2008.[2]. 120 pp.

*Articles on the Biblical and systematic fundament of World Mission, especially on mission as rooted in God's being, on 'Mission in the OT', and 'Romans as a Charter for World Mission'.*

Human Rights Threatened in Europe: Euthanasia – Abortion – Bioethicconvention. RVB International: Hamburg, 2001[1]; 2008.[2]. 100 pp.

*Updated Lectures on euthanasia and biomedicine at the 1st European Right to Life Forum Berlin, 1998, and articles on abortion.*

Be Keen to Get Going: William Careys Theology. RVB: Hamburg, 2001[1]; 2008[2]. 64 pp.

*First discussion of Carey's theology in length, explaining his Calvinistic and Postmillenial backround.*

Love is the Fulfillment of Love – Essays in Ethics. RVB: Hamburg, 2001[1]; 2008.[2]. 140 pp.

*Essays on ethical topics, including role of the Law, work ethics, and European Union.*

Mission und der Kampf um die Menschenrechte. RVB: Hamburg, 2001. 108 S.

[Mission and the Battle for Human Rights] *The relationship of world missions and the fight for human rights is discussed on an ethical level (theology of human rights) as well as on a practical level.*

The Persecution of Christians Concerns Us All: Towards a Theology of Martyrdom. At the same time Idea-Dokumentation 15/99 E. VKW: Bonn, 2001. 156 pp.

*70 thesis on persecution and martyrdom, written for the International Day of Prayer for the Persecuted Church on behalf of the German and European Evangelical Alliance*

Hope for Europe: 66 Theses. VTR: Nürnberg, 2002

*Official thesis and study of hope in the Old and New Testament for Hope for Europe of the European Ev. Alliance and Lausanne Europe. Also available in German, Czech, Dutch, Spanish, Romanian, Portuguese, French, Russian, Italian, Hungarian, Latvian.*

Thomas Schirrmacher, Christine Schirrmacher u. a. Harenberg Lexikon der Religionen. Harenberg Verlag: Düsseldorf, 2002. 1020 pp.

[Harenberg Dictionary of World Religions] In a major secular dictionary on world religions, Thomas Schirrmacher wrote the section on Christianity ('Lexicon of Christianity', pp. 8-267) and Christine Schirrmacher the section on Islam ('Lexicon of Islam', 'pp. 428-549).

Studies in Church Leadership: New Testament Church Structure – Paul and His Coworkers – An Alternative Theological Education – A Critique of Catholic Canon Law. VKW: Bonn, 2003[1]; RVB: Hamburg, 2008.[2]. 112 pp.

Hitlers Kriegsreligion: Die Verankerung der Weltanschauung Hitlers in seiner religiösen Begrifflichkeit und seinem Gottesbild. 2 vol. VKW: Bonn, 2007. 1220 pp.

[Hitlers Religion of War] *A research about the religious terms and thoughts in all texts and speeches of Hitler of Hitler, pleading for a new way of explaining Hitler's worldview, rise and breakdown.*

Moderne Väter: Weder Waschlappen, noch Despot. Hänssler: Holzgerlingen, 2007. 96 pp.

[Modern Fathers] Presents the result of international father research, explains the necessity of the father's involvement for his children and gives practical guidelines.

Internetpornografie. Hänssler: Holzgerlingen, 2008. 156 pp.

[Internet pornography] *Intense study of spread of pornography, its use amongst children and young people,* its *psychological results and dangers, including steps how to escape sex and pornography addiction.*

May a Christian Go to Court and other Essays on Persecution vs. Religious Freedom. WEA Global Issues Series. VKW: Bonn, 2008. 120 pp.

*Essays: "Is Involvement in the Fight Against the Persecution of Christians Solely for the Benefit of Christians?", "But with gentleness and respect: Why missions should be ruled by ethics". "May a Christian Go to Court?", "Putting Rumors to Rest", "Human Rights and Christian Faith", "There Has to Be a Social Ethic".*

Indulgences: A History of Theology and Reality of Indulgences and Purgatory. VKW: Bonn, 2011. 164 pp.

*History and theology of the Catholic view on indulgences.*

Thomas Schirrmacher, Richard Howell. Racism. With an essay on Caste in India. VKW: Bonn, 2011. 100 pp.

*History and scientific errors of racism*

Menschenrechte: Anspruch und Wirklichkeit. Holzgerlingen: SCM Hänssler, 2012. 120 pp.

[Human Rights]: *Ethical arguments for human rights versus the present stage of the violation of human rights worldwide.*

Christ and the Trinity in the Old Testament. Edited by James E. Anderson. RVB: Hamburg, 2013. 82 pp.

*On Christ and the Trinity in the Old Testament and on 'the Angel of the Lord'. Taken from 'Ethik'.*

## Selection from the books edited by the author:

Scham- und Schuldorientierung in der Diskussion: Kulturanthropologische, missiologische und theologische Einsichten (mit Klaus W. Müller). VTR: Nürnberg & VKW: Bonn, 2006

[Shame- and Guiltorientation] *A selection of experts from all continents on the difference between shame- and guiltoriented cultures and its implications for world missions.*

HIV und AIDS als christliche Herausforderung (mit Kurt Bangert). Verlag für Kultur und Wissenschaft: Bonn, 2008. 211 pp.

[HIV and AIDS as Christian Challenge] *Essay on how the Christian church should react to HIV and AIDS and how it does react. Published together with World Vision Germany.*

Der Kampf gegen die weltweite Armut – Aufgabe der Evangelischen Allianz? Zur biblisch-theologischen Begründung der Micha-Initiative. (with Andreas Kusch). VKW/Idea: Bonn, 2009. 230 pp.

[The fight against poverty – task of the Evangelical Alliance?] *Essays by theologians, missiologists, activists etc. in favour of the MICAH initiative of the World Evangelical Alliance.*

Tough-Minded Christianity: Honoring the Legacy of John Warwick Montgomery. (with William Dembski). (2009) B&H Academic Publ.: Nashville (TN). 830 pp.

*Large Festschrift with essays by many major Evangelical theologians and lawyers.*

Calvin and World Mission: Essays- VKW: Bonn, VTR: Nürnberg, 2009. 204 pp.

*Collection of essays from 1882 to 2002.*

# Biography

Prof. Dr. theol. Dr. phil. Thomas Schirrmacher, PhD, DD, (born 1960) is Ambassador for Human Rights of the World Evangelical Alliance, speaking for appr. 600 million Christians, chair of its Theological Commission, and director of its International Institute for Religious Freedom (Bonn, Cape Town, Colombo). He is also director of the Commission for Religious Freedom of the German and Austrian Evangelical Alliance. He is member of the board of the International Society for Human Rights.

Schirrmacher is professor of the sociology of religion at the State University of the West in Timisoara (Romania) and Distinguished Professor of Global Ethics and International Development at William Carey University in Shillong (Meghalaya, India). He is also president of 'Martin Bucer European Theological Seminary and Research Institutes' with small campuses in Bonn, Berlin, Zurich, Linz, Innsbruck, Prague, Istanbul, and Sao Paulo, where he teaches ethics and comparative religions.

He studied theology from 1978 to 1982 at STH Basel (Switzerland) and since 1983 Cultural Anthropology and Comparative Religions at Bonn State University. He earned a Drs. theol. in Missiology and Ecumenics at Theological University (Kampen/Netherlands) in 1984, and a Dr. theol. in Missiology and Ecumenics at Johannes Calvin Foundation (Kampen/Netherlands) in 1985, a Ph.D. in Cultural Anthropology at Pacific Western University in Los Angeles (CA) in 1989, a Th.D. in Ethics at Whitefield Theological Seminary in Lakeland (FL) in 1996, and a Dr. phil. in Comparative Religions / Sociology of Religion at State University of Bonn in 2007. In 1997 he received an honorary doctorate (D.D.) from Cranmer Theological House, in 2006 one from Acts University in Bangalore.

Schirrmacher regularly testifies in the German parliament and other parliaments in Europe, in the EU parliament in Brussels, the OSCE in Vienna and the UN Human Rights Council in Geneva.

He has written or edited 94 books on ethics, missiology and cultural anthropology, which were translated into 17 languages.

He is listed in Marquis' Who's Who in the World, Dictionary of International Biography, International Who is Who of Professionals, 2000 Outstanding Intellectuals of the 21st Century and many other biographical yearbooks.

*See more at www.thomasschirrmacher.net/eine-seite/biography.*

# World Evangelical Alliance

World Evangelical Alliance is a global ministry working with local churches around the world to join in common concern to live and proclaim the Good News of Jesus in their communities. WEA is a network of churches in 129 nations that have each formed an evangelical alliance and over 100 international organizations joining together to give a worldwide identity, voice and platform to more than 600 million evangelical Christians. Seeking holiness, justice and renewal at every level of society – individual, family, community and culture, God is glorified and the nations of the earth are forever transformed.

Christians from ten countries met in London in 1846 for the purpose of launching, in their own words, "a new thing in church history, a definite organization for the expression of unity amongst Christian individuals belonging to different churches." This was the beginning of a vision that was fulfilled in 1951 when believers from 21 countries officially formed the World Evangelical Fellowship. Today, 150 years after the London gathering, WEA is a dynamic global structure for unity and action that embraces 600 million evangelicals in 129 countries. It is a unity based on the historic Christian faith expressed in the evangelical tradition. And it looks to the future with vision to accomplish God's purposes in discipling the nations for Jesus Christ.

Commissions:

- Theology
- Missions
- Religious Liberty
- Women's Concerns
- Youth
- Information Technology

Initiatives and Activities

- Ambassador for Human Rights
- Ambassador for Refugees
- Creation Care Task Force
- Global Generosity Network
- International Institute for Religious Freedom
- International Institute for Islamic Studies
- Leadership Institute
- Micah Challenge
- Global Human Trafficking Task Force
- Peace and Reconciliation Initiative
- UN-Team

Church Street Station
P.O. Box 3402
New York, NY 10008-3402
Phone +[1] 212 233 3046
Fax +[1] 646-957-9218
www.worldea.org

## Giving Hands

GIVING HANDS GERMANY (GH) was established in 1995 and is officially recognized as a nonprofit foreign aid organization. It is an international operating charity that – up to now – has been supporting projects in about 40 countries on four continents. In particular we care for orphans and street children. Our major focus is on Africa and Central America. GIVING HANDS always mainly provides assistance for self-help and furthers human rights thinking.

The charity itself is not bound to any church, but on the spot we are co-operating with churches of all denominations. Naturally we also cooperate with other charities as well as governmental organizations to provide assistance as effective as possible under the given circumstances.

The work of GIVING HANDS GERMANY is controlled by a supervisory board. Members of this board are Manfred Feldmann, Colonel V. Doner and Kathleen McCall. Dr. Christine Schirrmacher is registered as legal manager of GIVING HANDS at the local district court. The local office and work of the charity are coordinated by Rev. Horst J. Kreie as executive manager. Dr. theol. Thomas Schirrmacher serves as a special consultant for all projects.

Thanks to our international contacts companies and organizations from many countries time and again provide containers with gifts in kind which we send to the different destinations where these goods help to satisfy elementary needs. This statutory purpose is put into practice by granting nutrition, clothing, education, construction and maintenance of training centers at home and abroad, construction of wells and operation of water treatment systems, guidance for self-help and transportation of goods and gifts to areas and countries where needy people live.

GIVING HANDS has a publishing arm under the leadership of Titus Vogt, that publishes human rights and other books in English, Spanish, Swahili and other languages.

These aims are aspired to the glory of the Lord according to the basic Christian principles put down in the Holy Bible.

Baumschulallee 3a • D-53115 Bonn • Germany
Phone: +49 / 228 / 695531 • Fax +49 / 228 / 695532
www.gebende-haende.de • info@gebende-haende.de

# Martin Bucer Seminary

**Faithful to biblical truth**
**Cooperating with the Evangelical Alliance**
**Reformed**

## Solid training for the Kingdom of God
- Alternative theological education
- Study while serving a church or working another job
- Enables students to remain in their own churches
- Encourages independent thinking
- Learning from the growth of the universal church.

## Academic
- For the Bachelor's degree: 180 Bologna-Credits
- For the Master's degree: 120 additional Credits
- Both old and new teaching methods: All day seminars, independent study, term papers, etc.

## Our Orientation:
- Complete trust in the reliability of the Bible
- Building on reformation theology
- Based on the confession of the German Evangelical Alliance
- Open for innovations in the Kingdom of God

## Our Emphasis:
- The Bible
- Ethics and Basic Theology
- Missions
- The Church

## Our Style:
- Innovative
- Relevant to society
- International
- Research oriented
- Interdisciplinary

## Structure
- 15 study centers in 7 countries with local partners
- 5 research institutes
- President: Prof. Dr. Thomas Schirrmacher
  Vice President: Prof. Dr. Thomas K. Johnson
- Deans: Thomas Kinker, Th.D.;
  Titus Vogt, lic. theol., Carsten Friedrich, M.Th.

## Missions through research
- Institute for Religious Freedom
- Institute for Islamic Studies
- Institute for Life and Family Studies
- Institute for Crisis, Dying, and Grief Counseling
- Institute for Pastoral Care

www.bucer.eu • info@bucer.eu

Berlin I Bielefeld I Bonn I Chemnitz I Hamburg I Munich I Pforzheim
Innsbruck I Istanbul I Izmir I Linz I Prague I São Paulo I Tirana I Zurich